How to Write an
ONLINE
OBITUARY

Virtual Memorials Made Simple

Melissa Jayne Kinsey

Nicholson
& Stillwell

Kinsey, Melissa Jayne

How to write an online obituary: Virtual memorials made simple /
by Melissa Jayne Kinsey

St. Louis, Missouri: Nicholson & Stillwell, 2017. | Summary: A guide
to obituary writing for the digital age, including preparation of
images, video, and music for use in virtual memorial sites and apps.

LCCN 2017908994 (print) | ISBN 978-0-9990520-2-0 (softcover) |
ISBN 978-0-9990520-3-7 (epub)

Obituaries -- authorship
Death -- social aspects
Creative writing -- technological innovations

LC record available at https://lccn.loc.gov/2017908994

Cover design: Marlon Joshua A. Namoro
Cover image: Copyright ©2015 CSA-Printstock

First edition.

Printed in the United States of America

*Thoughts? Ideas? Please post a review or get in touch directly:
melissa@HowtoWriteanOnlineObit.com.*

CONTENTS

ACKNOWLEDGMENTS

This book contains nearly 150 excerpts from real obituaries and virtual memorials. Each is accompanied by the deceased person's name and dates of birth and death. Typos in the excerpts have been corrected. An ellipsis appears where words have been omitted for space. Otherwise, the obit text is quoted verbatim. My thanks to the talented authors of these splendid tributes.

Special thanks to my friend and publishing mentor, Wayne A. Payne, whose warm encouragement and unflagging support helped me become a finisher, at least just this once; to LaJean Salonites, whose friendship kept up my spirits through the final stretch; to my husband, Brian, who remains The Most Interesting Man in the World and has been a mensch in all the ways that count; to my mother, who has loved every idea I've ever had, including this one, and who proved a remarkably good proofreader and critic; and to my father, who would've been tickled to know that his death had led me down this path.

A Message to Readers

Thank you in advance for your thoughtful reviews on Amazon, Goodreads, and elsewhere. I'm eager to know what you think! If you have questions or ideas, I'd love to hear them. Please drop me a line: melissa@HowtoWriteanOnlineObit.com.

PREFACE
Gone with the Wind

When my father died in 2014, my family and I discovered we'd have to pony up $600 to place an obituary in the paper. "Why not circulate it by email instead?" suggested my mother, then 72 years old. This idea was a surprise coming from her, since she's been known to ask what a "blue tooth" is and where, exactly, the cloud is located. She was familiar with email from having listened gamely every morning as my dad scrolled through his joke emails and read the good ones out loud to her.

"Perfect," I said. "I'll write it, and we'll send it to all of his contacts and post it online." I got started right away. Or tried to. But the weight of my grief and the scope the task unnerved me. Where to begin? My dad had served his country and had been a marvelous father and grandfather—but that description fit thousands of other men. Which stories would capture my dad's uniqueness? Which details could I offer to illustrate his curiosity, his steadfastness, his generosity and playfulness?

My father had led a remarkable life. He'd gone from slopping hogs on an Illinois farm to riding camels in Cairo, sampling pork satay in Bangkok, and cruising through restricted airspace over Tehran. He was a family man, too. For my older brother, he built treehouses and soap-box derby cars. He taught me how to ride a bike and how to drive, cringing each time I let out the clutch too fast and killed the engine. My folks took us camping and sailing and bowling. We went to museums and petting zoos and battlefields and Renaissance fairs—well, one Renaissance fair, which is enough for anyone.

My dad could be unreasonable, forbidding me at age 12 to watch *Gone with the Wind*—too racy, he said—and giving me an 11:00 curfew on senior prom night. But he was always there. He always picked up the phone. From 1,000 miles away, he'd walk me through any household repair or improvement, from replacing a doorbell to hanging a curtain rod. He brainstormed business names with me. He read everything I wrote.

It's those details that turn a name into a person. My dad deserved more than a bare-bones announcement of his passing—doesn't everyone? A dry recitation of schools, job titles, and "survivors" would be of interest only to some future genealogist.

My Google searches for guidance on crafting an obituary, though, taught me none of that. I turned up only predictable suggestions. The web has obliterated space limitations and media restrictions, yet obituary writers are urged to follow the same shopworn templates folks used 30 years ago. This advice makes as much sense as telling a digital photographer to conserve his film and flashbulbs.

During my 20-year career in medical publishing, I saw a similar shift occur. E-books and online learning became more and more sophisticated every year. At first the digital content was supplemental, but eventually it began to replace heavy, outdated textbooks. Producing dynamic new content required creativity, flexibility, and imagination. Simply digitizing the printed page wasn't enough. Publishers who didn't get that were left behind.

Likewise, an online obituary must be more than just a digitized death notice. The electronic format has made it possible for anyone to create a richly illustrated tribute and share it on social media. New memorial sites and apps (see Chapter 8) facilitate collaboration, allowing multiple users to post media and start conversations. These innovative options are encouraging many people to write their own send-offs. A written obituary still lies at the heart of most tributes (see Chapter 5), but its content has been transformed from chilly and formulaic to thoughtful, intimate, and often funny.

I knew none of this as I sat down to write my dad's obituary. Casting about for direction but finding little, I applied what I knew of writing in general and waded chest-deep into my churning thoughts. When I finished and the piece was posted, those who had known my dad—some of whom he'd lost touch with decades ago—began to respond. Many said they'd learned something new about him. A few attached photos we'd never seen. Others remarked that his unlikely journey had inspired them to reflect on their own choices: "I read about everything your dad did and all the places he went," said one, "and I asked myself, 'What the heck have *you* done with *your* time?'"

—

"If there's a book you really want to read, but it hasn't been written yet, then you must write it," said National Book Award winner Toni Morrison. *How to Write an Online Obituary* is the guide I wish I'd had when I sat down to write my dad's obit. It replaces the paint-by-numbers approach with simple, flexible steps for crafting a fresh, compelling online obit or virtual memorial.

This book is not aimed at the professional writer who's turning out tributes for luminaries, dignitaries…*personages*. It's for ordinary people—those who wish to remember a parent or child, partner or spouse, brother or sister, friend, pastor, teacher, mentor, or fallen soldier, and for those who would rather not leave their own obituaries to chance.

"No one is useless in this world who lightens the burden of another," said Charles Dickens. It's my sincere hope that in writing this book, I've made myself useful. Our loved ones may be gone with the wind, but let's give them a grand send-off, shall we?

Chapter 1

NOT YOUR GRANDFATHER'S OBITUARY
Scrapping the Assembly-Line Tribute

For generations, Americans read the obituary page in the morning and wrapped up their coffee grounds and potato peelings in it that evening. The wife or daughter of the deceased might clip the piece and save it for posterity, but everyone else in town tossed it out with the garbage.

YESTERDAY'S OBIT

Newspaper obituaries were heavy, solemn pieces freighted with scripture and offering little more than a few humdrum facts about the deceased. Clichés abounded: The dearly departed likely died peacefully, often in his sleep and/or surrounded by family. He was always headed for some swell immortal abode, where his loved ones would soon—but not too soon—join him. There he would receive his heavenly reward—a band of angels,

1

perhaps, or the proverbial 72 virgins. (Personally, I'd settle for one or two shirtless Dothrakis.)

Comforting images of pearly gates and puffy clouds served as window dressing for these black-and-white death notices—serviceable pieces as predictable and rigidly structured as the Sunday mass. They spread the word that old lady Vierheller's rent-controlled flat was up for grabs, or that Earl Maynard's feuding sons now had 400 acres and a Deere to squabble over. A boilerplate template governed the obit's format and content. Rarely did the resulting tribute capture the uniqueness of the deceased—let's call him or her the "obituee."

THE OBITUARY GETS ITS GROOVE ON

Obituaries tend to reflect current cultural values and historical realities. Those written during the Great Depression and during the Vietnam era, for example, emphasized perseverance. World War II–era obits were often pensive, sad, and sentimental. These minor variations aside, the obituary remained straightlaced, humorless, and strangely generic for decades.

Then the internet changed everything. The obituary stripped off its starched shirt and slipped into a more comfortable style. This new, modern tribute celebrates our individuality, takes stock of our accomplishments, stands as a memorial to our life and times, and encourages sharing (see Chapter 2).

The obituary's extreme makeover has been part of a larger shift in our approach to death and dying. "Obituaries are rituals," writes sociologist Jason B. Phillips. "Accordingly, if the attitudes and practices that surround death change[,] we would expect the presentation of death to change in these rituals."[1] Three related trends have driven this transformation:

- **Declining faith.** Over the past several decades, the influence of faith has waned. The bright shiny thing that holds our attention now is life—not the afterlife.
- **Confessional climate.** Today's aspirational, narcissistic culture encourages us to tell our stories and share (some might say *overshare*) our experiences, thoughts, and ideas via social media.

2

- **Advancing technology.** The web has given us innovative new ways to express ourselves. It's allowed us to connect with one another using mobile devices, social media, and apps for creating, recording, and sharing photos, videos, games, podcasts, and music.

In the remainder of the chapter, we'll take a look at each of these trends. If you just want to get started already, skip to Chapter 2.

Facebook Is the New Faith

We rely on our digital connections to nurture friendships, meet like-minded people, and exchange everything from recipes and DIY tips to snippets of code. Social networks have seamlessly, perhaps insidiously, replaced the bonds we once formed within our houses of worship.

We've traded ice cream socials for subreddits and Twitter followers. These so-called micro–affinity groups are composed of social media users closely matched in age, gender, ethnicity, and life experience. Virtual communities have formed, for example, among collectors of everything from sports-themed cereal boxes to vintage HoJo placemats. There are Trekkies who text in Klingon and Harry Potter fans who play virtual Quidditch. These groups give a whole new meaning to the phrase "community of faith."

All Dogs Go to Heaven

The idea that religious faith is weakened by modernization is known as the "secularization thesis." I can hear all those books and iPad cases snapping shut, but stay with me, now. This'll just take a sec to explain. According to this theory, sacred beliefs and secular (meaning non-religious) ideas lie at opposite poles.[2] As we move toward one, we move away from the other. In other words, we grow ever more distant from our spiritual beliefs as scientists decode our epigenome, train robots for combat and companionship, 3D print our homes and organs, and finally figure out why dogs eat grass.

Will faith be trampled beneath the goosestep of progress? Let's just say things aren't looking good for the apostles.

According to an epic 2014 Pew Research Center study,[3] nearly one third of Americans now consider themselves to be "nones"—in other words, religious doubters, free agents, or flat-out heathens. "We are all atheists about most of the gods that humanity has ever believed in," says British biologist Richard Dawkins. "Some of us just go one god further."[4]

Evidence of waning religious sentiment crops up in curious places. The greeting card business, which depends on its ability to predict cultural trends, spotted this one early and began to capitalize on it. The industry quietly started to introduce card lines that might once have been offensive.[5] Consumers have so eagerly embraced the idea of sending pet condolences, for example, that doggie sympathy cards now seem normal. Think about that a minute.

A Good Death

Evolving attitudes toward death are apparent even among the dying. Rarely do terminally ill people linger in hospital rooms, awaiting the inevitable. Many choose instead to enroll in home hospice care. They invite their contacts to follow their medical ups and downs on caringbridge.com. They announce their diagnoses on Facebook and post a self-nado of pics on Instagram from the chemo room or dialysis lounge.

With obvious exceptions, death isn't as sobering an event as it once was. Much of the credit goes to the hospice care movement, which has both responded to and helped shape our perception of what a "good death" means. Most hospice patients die in their own homes. Family satisfaction with hospice care is an astonishing 98%.[6] For many, hospice offers dying patients and their families the comfort that earlier generations found in their faith. As a result, we're that much less connected to our religious institutions. For more on the influence of the hospice movement, visit HowtoWriteanOnlineObit.com.

Scatter My Ashes at Old Navy

The way we dress for funerals mirrors our changing views on death and dying. A century ago, mourning attire was considered a religious observance. These days, your average funeral guest might be mistaken for a patron of the local pub or bowling alley. In keeping with the modern view of death as a celebration of life, we steer clear of formal, somber funeral garb. James "Jim" Groth's obit warns, tongue in cheek, that "[a]nyone wearing black will not be admitted to the memorial."

Sometimes guests are asked to dress in the favorite color or style of the departed. The obituary for 17-year-old Clayton "Clay" Samuel Tully, who died of injuries sustained in an Idaho car crash, offers a bittersweet example: "Those knew him, knew he was never about being fancy. We would like to honor him by asking all who attend the funeral to wear either a plaid button-up shirt or camouflage."

Customized Demise

A modern funeral departs from the rigid sequence of a bleak hymn followed by an invocation, Bible readings, and prayers. Hymns and holy water have given way to slide shows and stories. It's telling that the bureaucratic-sounding word "officiant" has been superseded by the term "celebrant."

With religious considerations having moved to the sidelines, everything from headstones to hearses is being customized and personalized—Americanized, you might say. The mood is celebratory, rather than sad. If the deceased was cremated, his or her cremains are usually placed in an engraved urn (or in a vintage Coleman jug, if my cousin Joe's wishes are honored).

According to the National Funeral Directors Association (NFDA), the number of families choosing cremation in the United States increased from one-third of burials in 2005 to nearly half in 2015. That year, for the first time, more people in this country were cremated (48%) than buried (45%).[7] (The NFDA is mum on the fate of the remaining 7% of corpses.)

Cremation allows the funeral or memorial service to be delayed, which has several advantages. It gives mourners the opportunity to grieve and adjust to the loss before friends and family come together. It gives loved ones more time to plan a memorial that truly celebrates the individual's unique qualities—

perhaps even a "destination funeral." And foregoing an immediate service gives the obituary writer time to collect information, prepare the obit, and choose, find, or create complementary media. See Chapters 3 and 4 for more information on preparing to write, and see Chapter 9 for advice on sourcing media.

Confessional Culture

Although losing a loved one remains wrenching, we no longer say farewell with somber ceremonies. Priests and prelates are still a welcome presence at many services, and their wisdom can bring great comfort. But families expect the message to be personal. We want to remember our loved ones as they were.

This cultural shift is evident in the modern obituary. Instead of relying on euphemisms, we admit our loved ones' flaws with humor and compassion. Some obits share painful truths about mental illness, addiction, or other serious challenges. America's confessional climate has allowed us to drop the pretense of perfection.

In fact, we've revealed so much that it's hard to remember a time when it was shocking for bladder control products to be advertised on television or for Bob Dole to reveal his erectile dysfunction publicly, as he did in 1999. Americans have been privy to the shame and desperation of addicted people and their families on *Intervention* and *Celebrity Rehab*. We've contemplated kink camp and balloon fetishes on podcasts like *Risk!* and the *Savage Lovecast*. How did we get here?

This kind of candidness was encouraged, first of all, by improvements in production equipment and handheld videocam technology. These innovations made it possible to capture a gritty realism in documentary series like *Cops*. As competition escalated between network shows and cable channels, TV producers adopted tabloid tactics to cover scandalous topics.[8] The result was talk shows like *Ricki Lake, Oprah, Howard Stern,* and *Geraldo,* infotainment such as *America's Most Wanted,* docudramas like *16 and Pregnant,* and so-called reality TV shows such as *The Bachelor.*

"Suddenly no episode was too sordid, no family too dysfunctional to be trotted out for the wonderment of the masses in books and magazines and on talk shows," observed William Zinsser, an authority on the craft of memoir.[9] Those wanna-be baby daddies on *The Jerry Springer Show* probably didn't set out to be trailblazers, but they and others like them opened the door to what writer Laura Bennett calls the "first-person industrial complex," in which bloggers and writers offer up their most intimate insecurities and woes for public consumption.[10]

The web itself, of course, provides a sense of safety and anonymity that encourages sharing. According to Google Trends data, the term "oversharing" was coined around 2004 and quickly entered popular parlance.[11] (Searches for the term, by the way, are most often followed by the words "on Facebook." Just sayin'.) It's possible to overshare in an obituary, too (see Chapter 7 for advice on handling delicate situations).

Traditional obituaries err in the opposite direction. They gloss over glaring flaws and ignore human failings. Every dead guy or gal appears to have been a saint who skipped through life down a path strewn with daisies, encountering nary a bad hair day. Modern obituaries are, ideally, more candid and balanced. Stephen Lock, editor of the *British Medical Journal,* believes it's important to give "the truth about a rounded human being with his or her foibles as well as achievements."[12]

Modern obit writers—let's call them obituarists—celebrate the obituee as a real, three-dimensional person: "Jim could be stubborn at times and was sometimes impossible to live with," admits the 2013 obituary for James L. Bullock, who helped shape the assisted living industry. Bullock "rarely took no for an answer. He was impatient and his timing was not always the best. Jim deplored dealing with the details and didn't suffer boredom easily." Just as you're beginning to either feel sorry for the bloke or write him off as a heartless clod, however, the obituary softens: "These characteristics, which some might consider flaws, made Jim's life the adventure it was and led him to surround himself with people who cared, who could handle the details, and who appreciated sharing the journey."

Advancing Technology

At the turn of the millennium, few could have predicted the extent to which technology would transform our lives. According to Pew research, in 2000, only 37% of Americans had home internet connections—nearly all of them dial-up. Steve Jobs wouldn't unveil the first iPhone for another 7 years. Social media, tablet computers, e-book readers, and portable gaming devices did not yet exist. There was no Facebook, no Wikipedia, no Netflix or YouTube. Amazon.com was just a bookstore. Nevertheless, Americans recognized that a great change had been set in motion.

Obits Without Borders

Back in the day, there were two kinds of obituaries: Death notices were paid public announcements written by a mortuary employee, a family member, or even a classified ads clerk. News obits—tributes to powerbrokers and plutocrats—were written by staff reporters, usually without a byline. Such pieces were often prepared long before the A-lister in question had perished.

Technology has pixelated the formerly clear line between news obituaries and death notices. Once YouTube caught on, any bystander with a cell phone camera could call himself a journalist. Americans lost interest in scripted language and slick broadcasts delivered by well-coiffured reporters bearing fur-covered microphones. We found it much more entertaining to watch shaky jump cuts posted by a guy with a crush on Harry Styles. "Where our existing information systems seek to choke the flow of information through taboos, costs, and restrictions," wrote Jon Katz in a prescient 1997 *Wired* magazine piece, "the new digital world celebrates the right of the individual to speak and be heard—one of the cornerstone ideas behind American media and democracy."[13]

Likewise, sites like LiveJournal (launched in 1999) and Wordpress (launched in 2003) allowed anyone to become a published writer. When Blogger was launched in 1999, only about half of Americans used the internet.[14] Across this digital divide, folks struggled to wrap their heads around the concept of blogging. A blog is a "cyber bulletin board," Tim Russert explained to perplexed viewers in 2004. At first, late-night comedians snickered at the image of an overnourished blogger hacking away in the basement of his parents' split-level. In short order, however, photogenic young bloggers began to appear alongside credible Ivy League panelists on *Meet the Press* and *Fox News Sunday*. Colorful opinions and short skirts carried the day.

Out of Print

Meanwhile, computers continued to get smaller, lighter, faster, and cheaper. Mobile access became almost universal in developed countries. Early concern about the legality of linking to others' content—or using it outright—receded even when it shouldn't have.

Within two decades, Craigslist virtually wiped out classified ad revenue, hobbling the entire newspaper industry. Some papers tried to protect their online content behind paywalls, but most have had to settle for a more permeable barrier, allowing access to a certain amount of free content before imposing a fee or requiring a subscription. Some publications, such as the German daily *Bild,* shield their content only from those with ad blockers installed on their devices.

Online tabloid papers like the *National Enquirer* and the *Daily Mail* generate site traffic with titillating content—crime stories, conspiracy theories, celebrity gossip and such. They also reel in visitors with masterful headlines: "The Easy Diet Everyone's Talking About," "8 Mistakes That Will Destroy Your Marriage," "The Little White Lie That Will Transform Your Sex Life," and "Easy Ways to Find Out What Your Boss Really Thinks of You."

This kind of clickbait yields healthy response rates and generates a high volume of social media shares, both of which attract ad dollars. Nevertheless, digital ad revenue has been hard for newspapers to come by. Many advertisers blow their marketing wads on Facebook and Google AdWords.[15] Thanks to oversharing, such ads tend to be effective because they target the right demographic. Facebook and Google also give advertisers prime opportunities to run video ads (recall that Google owns YouTube).

The popularity of online obituary sites has spawned mobile apps and subscription-based memorial websites, discussed at length in Chapter 8. These multimedia platforms allow us to memorialize loved ones and interact with our social networks, making the static newspaper obituary seem antiquated by comparison. If "commemoration is ultimately expected to be a public affair," concludes author Michael Arntfield, obituaries are "much too important to be left to the sole discretion of newspapermen."[16]

Chapter 2

RANDOM ACCESS MEMORIES
The Mission of the Modern Obit

When we're young, life looks like a tidy picnic hamper packed with our hopes and dreams. We expect the basket to yield up all manner of delights each time open it. Often it does. But every now and then, something spoils in the heat. A contemporary obituary acknowledges these misfortunes and poor choices, letting life's disappointments and our own foul-ups humanize us.

Today's obituary makes "a fresh set of calculations about what an exemplary or memorable life is," says historian Bridget Fowler.[1] Miscalculations, blunders, and gaffes are part of the package. We no longer buff out all those flaws with a shiny coat of Turtle Wax. Instead, we showcase an obituee's individuality, recall his accomplishments, and capture the moment in which he lived. Online obits bring us stories of ordinary people, written by those who knew and loved them.

CELEBRATING OUR INDIVIDUALITY

Australian physician Ben Haneman got so fed up reading florid obits for his late colleagues that he published an opinion piece on the topic in a popular medical journal:

> Reading again and again of irreparable losses, of never again seeing a man of such virtue and skill grace the medical profession, of leadership positions that would never be so well filled in the future, it seems a miracle that the profession has survived at all.[2]

Be kind but candid about the obituee's faults, Haneman said: "A modicum of cynicism makes for more interesting reading." Insincerity, egotism, obstinacy—every foible is fair game.

Dr. Haneman's article appeared in January 2001. In December of that year, he died suddenly. Three colleagues wrote obits for him, all brimming with praise. One even called the good doctor "irreplaceable." Apparently they had a little reading to catch up on.

I wrote my mother's pre-need obituary in preparation for this book (see Chapter 6 for the full obit). As I write this a few months before her 75th birthday, she's trim, energetic, and in perfect health. She and I have always been close, and I'd assumed that if my dad died before she did, we'd become even closer.

Three years ago, my father developed heart failure and died after a few weeks in home hospice care. Alone for the first time in her life, my mom wanted to see herself as an independent widow. After all, she wasn't feeble or timid or sickly. She refused to wallow in self-pity. What good would it do? No, better to suppress those silly tears, keep a Churchillian upper lip, and get on with it.

Yet it was clear she wasn't ready to be by herself. My teenage nephew moved in with her almost immediately, and she was utterly absorbed in his welfare for the next three years. As I wrote about this transition in her obituary, I tried to keep events in perspective and aim for what Wordsworth called "truth hallowed by love":

After Dick died, Richard Philip moved in with Judy, and she home-schooled him until his high school graduation three years later. The two were inseparable, leaving little room for Judy to grieve. But that's how she wanted it. With an Englishwoman's disdain of weakness, she refused to entertain the slightest pang of loneliness or heartache.

My mother's self-imposed insularity during that time was more a blind spot than a fault, but I had to include it if I wanted my portrait of her to be genuine. See Chapter 6 for the full obituary.

An acknowledgment of your obituee's human frailties acts as a foil to your praise, making it more authentic. When Jack Sullivan died in 2012, for example, his daughter Cheryl wrote a tender tribute that includes this gentle aside:

> Our relationship wasn't always perfect. He would get me mad and I would go to his pantry, which was neatly organized just like a grocery store, and turn all the labels and mix up the cans! Now that was payback! *—John "Jack" Sullivan (1933–2012)*

Or take this example from one of my favorite obits:

> Dad was a huge risk taker and loved to occasionally gamble at the casinos and horse tracks. Investing in the stock market and playing options was a huge interest. On one family vacation Dad gambled and lost all the vacation funds. *—Raymond Benet (Benoit Raymond Benezra, 1918–2010)*

The rest of the piece presents Mr. Benet as a prosperous entrepreneur and devoted family man. This hint that he might have been a little too fond of rolling the dice tells us only that he was human. Here's another candid yet kind tribute:

> John had a unique artistic sensibility and could quickly create what was simple and elegant in tile, wood, or stone. His sometimes bristly surface masked a heart both sensitive and kind to all living creatures. A highlight of his life was planting a kiss on a baby whale that surfaced near him in the waters off Baja, CA. *—John W. McGurk (1946–2012)*

13

Even the most successful person has limitations, as this tribute acknowledges:

> Tullia failed to do one thing: she never learned to drive an automobile. One can only speculate as to what she might have achieved if she hadn't been limited to traveling on foot in a world where everyone else traveled by automobile. *–Tullia Barbanti (1928–2016)*

We all know people who have trouble saying "I love you" or demonstrating physical affection. Is that a flaw or just a difference? In any case, this obit addresses the trait without judgment:

> Though he might not have expressed it vocally, family and friends were dear to his heart. It was shown in his quiet support to bring relatives to the U.S., and send others to school. It was shown in his association with his hometown U.S. organizations…It was also shown…in the forming of his retiree group at McDonald's; the McBuddies…. *–Tomas Solatorio Malunes (1928–2015)*

TAKING STOCK

An obituary, says Garrison Keillor, "reminds us that we too are mortal and someday the world will look at us with a cool[,] clear eye and measure our contribution to the common good."[3] Now, if that doesn't scare the bejesus out of you, you've lived a more virtuous life than I.

Professor Michael Locke puts the point more mildly, describing an obituary as a sort of balance sheet of a person's life. It tells us what he contributed, what we owe him, and what difference he made in the world.[4] Jim Nicholson, former obits editor for the *Philadelphia Daily News,* agrees: "Obituaries bring the deceased out onto the public stage, many for the first and only time, to give them a grand goodbye and in effect, decree to all the readers that this was a life well lived."[5]

STANDING IN MEMORIAM

An online obituary becomes a digital time capsule—"history writ small," said John Locke.[6] Taken together, our obituaries—

and now our virtual memorials, too—form a collective memory that will show future generations what interested us as a society, what we valued, and what challenges we faced. Terence Mickey, host of the popular podcast Memory Motel, compares the effect to that of a pointillist painting. "[A] thousand obituaries somehow give us the cultural landscape," he says.[7]

Places

Obituaries not only reflect our collective memory, but also help shape it. Our recollection of important places and events preserves a "little slice of local life," says newspaper editor Charles McCollum.[8] Take, for example, the Main Street Pier in Daytona Beach, Florida. We learn from Marjorie "Joan" Hulbert's obituary that in the late 1920s and '30s, she performed at the pier with her father's band, "Eddie's Dixie Aces." Her tribute conjures up a picture of the sand, the setting sun, and the handsome young couples streaming onto the pier for an evening of jitterbugging. Fast forward to December 7, 1941, and we find Cecelia Burch standing on the pier as she learns that Pearl Harbor has been attacked. Soon afterward, according to the obit, Burch moved to Memphis to work in an aircraft factory, where she helped build B-25 bombers for the war.

In the 1960s, we find Brett Gerken fishing off the pier and hanging out at Ramsey's Tackle Shop nearby. Gerken eventually became captain of a charter fishing boat on Daytona Beach.

A decade later, Jimmy Dyer's family took a road trip that ended at the Daytona Beach Pier. Little Jimmy's parents wanted the view to be a surprise, so when they got close, they told the kids to crouch down on the floorboard until they said the word:

> When [the kids] got up, [they] saw the ocean for the first time. They were parked on Daytona Beach at the Pier. It made such a lasting impression that Jimmy spent his entire adult life living and working in beach towns. –Jimmy Dyer (~1954–2013)

You'd be hard pressed to find a historian who could convey what the pier has meant to the Daytona Beach community more vividly than this handful of obituaries does.

Events

For better or worse, obituaries not only record history, but also help shape our view of it. One recent study, for example, looked at news obits written during the Civil Rights era.[9] Taken together, they immerse us in the conflict and tension of the time. Better than any wire service, they capture the emotions that drive human actions: arrogance and humility, cowardice and courage, ugliness and grace, hubris and hope. Take this account of the 1962 riots sparked by racial integration at the University of Mississippi:

> …Al wore one of the white helmets seen in the many photographs of the riots. However, his helmet sported a stripe to allow his squad to follow his movements through the greenish tear gas… All the while Al kept a calm demeanor, even smiling at the crowds to keep them calm as possible. –*Clarence A. "Al" Butler (1929–2012)*

Generational Mood

Millennials, flower children, Baby Boomers, flappers—each generation has a shared set of cultural references. They grew up with the same music, wore the same fashions, communicated by the same means, and lived through the same events:

> Marge and her best friend Jeanne Wurtz decided to move to Chicago and seek their fortunes…When they arrived in Chicago, they found that the hotel reservations they had were preempted by soldiers returning home from WWII…[They] arrived back in town and snuck into a dance…trying to stay in the shadows out of embarrassment for being back so soon. –*Marjorie M. (Mattson) Bristol (1927–2010)*

As a Gen-Xer, I wasn't alive when Kennedy was shot but recall where I was when I learned of Princess Diana's fatal car crash (look her up, kids). I saw Star Wars and E.T. in theaters when they premiered. My running playlist includes R.E.O. Speedwagon and Journey and Queen. I'm appalled when people in their 20s tell me they've never heard of Freddie Mercury.

Even the hippest Millennial will eventually find her- or himself in this mortifying position. He'll hear some smug *après*-Millennial refer to Beyoncé's catalog as "oldies." He'll see Rihanna and Katy Perry in Poise ads. His own kids will make fun of his tattoo sleeves.

Think about your obituee's generation. What did they eat and drink? What did they watch, listen to, wear, and worry about? Where did they go, and how did they get there? Who were their icons, and what were their defining moments?

Individuals can't be pigeonholed, of course, but each generation tends to share similar values. Compare, say, the Greatest Generation with the Millennials. "My grandfather fought in World War II," says comedian Matt Donaher. "I had a panic attack during the series finale of Breaking Bad."

Most of the Greatest Generation is gone. Those in their seventies or eighties today belong to the so-called Silent Generation, which spans the Korean and Vietnam war eras. This generation was brought up to follow orders without questioning who gave them or why. They came of age in a naïve time, before WikiLeaks, Watergate, and racist Pepe.

In other words, their life choices weren't made in a vacuum. They were influenced by generational norms, historical events, and the cultural mood. "A good obit writer has to communicate the significance of a person, a place, an era," says Marilyn Johnson, author of *Dead Beat*.[10] Placing your obituee's life in this context helps you show, not just tell, her story. It also deposits another bit of wisdom into the lockbox of collective memory.

Cultural Climate

The cultural climate is the way of life characteristic of a certain era—it's the mood of the period. Of course, generational context and the cultural climate overlap. The difference is that everyone immersed in the cultural milieu experiences it, no matter which generation they belong to.

The cultural zeitgeist is often recognizable in an obit even if the time period is unspecified. In the following passage, for example, we know right away that it's the late '70s or early '80s:

In high school, Alan [sold] floppy disks to students in his computer class and club, developing an interface to allow Albany high schools to use existing Teletype machines as printers for newly acquired Radio Shack TRS 80 computers... –*Alan Ackerman (1963–2016)*

Time, place, values, and events sometimes coalesce into a cultural microclimate. This single paragraph from Alfredo Alonso's obituary, for instance, captures the upheaval, resourcefulness, and—ultimately—the prosperity of a typical American immigrant in the mid-20th century:

[He was born in] the northern Spanish province of Galicia…Surviving war-torn Spain, he left for New York via Norfolk, Virginia, in the late 1950s…He attended night school to learn English while he worked at Schrafft's Ice Cream in Brooklyn…and soon saved enough to buy Charlie's, a butcher shop located in the Bronx that he later expanded to include a grocery store. –*Alfredo Alonso (1926–2016)*

Military service is an important aspect of many obituees' life stories. If your obituee was a veteran, request his or her records from the National Archives (archives.gov/veterans). (To do so, you must be an immediate family member.) You might be surprised what you can learn from such records. They're a fascinating addition to a memorial site, too—just scan and post them as you would a photo. Be sure to obscure any personal information that could be exploited, such as the obituee's Social Security number.

Most veterans' obits offer name, rank (or "rate," as it's called in the U.S. Navy), branch of service, and perhaps the location or theater of war in which the obituee served:

He was a U.S. Navy veteran of World War II and a veteran of the Korean War serving in the Army. –*Edward Harold Anderson (~1926–2016)*

I'll bet Anderson had some colorful stories, but we don't have the pleasure of reading them. The description of his service is like a grainy black-and-white snapshot compared with the Technicolor vividness of the excerpt below. Mr. Cyr's obit is illustrated perfectly by an old photo of him in a spiffy white peaked cap:

> In 1966, Bob was sent to Russian language training school in Washington, D.C., [and] then assigned as a Russian interpreter at the Naval Communications Facility, Adak, Alaska…[At a later post] he was privy to the highest-level diplomatic messages at the time of the Bay of Pigs, and construction of the Berlin Wall.
> –*Robert Thomas "Bob" Cyr (1937–2016)*

ORDINARY PEOPLE

In a traditional obituary, cost, space limitations, a rigid style, and editorial censorship muffle the voice of the average person. Content is often confined to housekeeping details, such as date and place of death, funeral arrangements, and a list of surviving family members. In a print obituary, it's unlikely we'd learn, for instance, that Lydia Campbell Lerma liked to dance in high heels and drink shots of tequila. We wouldn't discover that Madonna McCannon, who enjoyed playing bingo and buying Scratchers tickets, was also an "active Nudist" (hey, I don't judge). And James Bullock's "brief stint as an agent for a blue grass band" would have gone unrecorded, his Gump-like shrimpboating and goldmining adventures forgotten.

But the online platform has freed the obituary from its black-and-white straightjacket. Obituary editors have discovered that readers are keenly interested in the lives of regular folks. Today's obit editors are less likely to celebrate Kennebunkport, Wall Street, and Pentagon types and more likely to spotlight your average Joe.

In October 2015, the *New York Times* published an obituary, of sorts, for George Bell.[11] Mr. Bell, a friendless hoarder, had died in Queens with more than half a million dollars in assets to his name. The *Times*'s 8,000-word story was a surprise sensation. It went viral and was read by more than 3 million people.

The Bell piece wasn't an obituary per se. Its focus veered away from Bell at times in order to explain, for instance, how

New York City settles the affairs of decedents with no living family members. But other than its length and these brief asides, there's little to distinguish the piece from a modern obituary—and this one held mobile readers' attention for an astonishing 6 minutes, on average. The *Times* and other papers got the message: Everyone has a story worth telling.

Chapter 3

SELFIE-REFLECTION
Autobituaries & Other Angsty Topics

When the brilliant mathematician Carl Friedrich Gauss was informed that his wife was dying, he replied, "Ask her to wait a moment—I am almost done." Unfortunately, the grim reaper works more like a Milan taxi than an Uber. You're not sure when your ride will show up, but once it gets there, the driver's not going to wait around while you finish packing your bags.

New York Times obituary writer Alden Whitman believed that "masterful obituaries, like fine funerals, must be planned well in advance."[1] You may be writing an obituary in anticipation of your own death or that of a loved one—let's borrow a funeral industry term and call it a "pre-need" obit. Or perhaps you have a loved one who has just died, and you're writing a tribute "at need." Either way, it helps to consider a few questions up front. How much time do you have to finish the piece? Who will write it or collaborate with you? Is it a good idea to write your own obituary? How long will your tribute be, and what tone will you use? This chapter will help you sort through those decisions.

WHAT'S YOUR DEADLINE?

Susan Little, an obituary hobbyist (yeah, that's a thing), wants to be ready when the Grim Reaper comes a-callin'. She's written an obituary for every member of her family, including herself and her children.[2]

If you have better things to do with your weekends, don't worry. An online obituary can be posted weeks or months after the Prince of Darkness takes his leave. There's no newspaper deadline to meet. Take some time to grieve. When you've had your fill of Netflix and Chinese takeout and you've grown weary of Talkspace and Farmville and good ol' fashioned moping, you can draft an obit and build a virtual memorial (see Chapter 8) over an extended period.

If you prefer a more cut-and-dried task, or you'd like to post a tribute before your obituee's funeral, the information in this book will help you prepare a quick barf draft (see Chapter 5) and get it ready for prime time. Later, like a *Chopped* contestant who's left her gummyfish granita in the blast chiller, you may recall a story or detail you wish you'd included. Fortunately, most online platforms are flexible enough to accommodate such changes.

In hindsight, I'd have done a number of things differently in my father's obit—I'd leave out the unwieldy list of surviving extended family members, for example, since that information is available elsewhere. But I wrote the best tribute I could in the brief period I had to devote to it—about 3 days—and I'm sure my dad would have liked it.

WHO SHOULD PREPARE THE OBITUARY TEXT?

Memorializing A Loved One

Preparing an obituary gives you a chance to reflect on the obituee's accomplishments and speak to those who knew him or her. This process can be therapeutic, particularly for nonbelievers who take little comfort in religious rituals. "[Losing a loved one] is like walking up the stairs to your bedroom in the dark, and thinking there is one more stair than there is," says author and all-around wise man Lemony Snicket. "Your foot falls down, through the air, and there is a sickly moment of dark surprise as you try and readjust the way you thought of things."[3]

Writing an obituary may be too much for you, especially if your loved one's death came without warning. If the task can't be delayed (see the previous section), recruit the help of a sympathetic friend or extended family member, or ask your mortuary director for help. Then share this book, along with any other resources you've discovered. If you're up to it, supply the writer with photos, video files, artwork, and other media to complement the obituary text (see Chapter 9).

Leaving your loved one's obituary in someone else's hands is risky, of course. One man who later enrolled in an obituary-writing class said he'd been disappointed with his wife's tribute. The man had felt too broken to write it himself, so he'd asked a family member to handle it: "[The obituarist] left out a lot of information he just couldn't figure out how to include at the time."[4] But standing in the headwind of your grief might take everything you have, and you shouldn't hesitate to ask for help. Your loved one would understand.

Memorializing an Estranged Family Member

Deciding who will write the obituary is tricky if you had a rocky relationship with the obituee. Along with or instead of grief, you may feel bitterness, frustration, anger, and perhaps guilt or remorse about things you did or didn't say or do. Toss a few sibling squabbles and intergenerational conflicts into the mix, and you've got some serious angst.

Those who have no quarrel with the obituee may object to an unflattering portrayal of him or her. Be sensitive if it seems appropriate, but don't be cowed by others' disapproval. "You're under no obligation to ask all your brothers and sisters and cousins how they remember [something]. There's no one authorized version of the shared past," says William Zinsser.[5]

Should you kick a guy when he's...well, six feet under? Maybe. Only you, as the obituarist, can decide whether to put lipstick on the pig. The important thing is to draw a portrait you can stand by. See Chapter 7 for more on handling sensitive situations.

Collaborating on an Obit

Sometimes two or more people work together on an obituary. The memorial page for Richard Lee Tripp, who died in 2006, for example, was "[p]repared by loving wife, family, and classmates."

To produce a seamless obit like Mr. Tripp's, have one person prepare a draft and circulate it to others. The Track Changes feature in Microsoft Word and sharing apps like Dropbox and Google Drive work well for this kind of round-robin approach. Don't forget to ask collaborators to upload photos and other memorabilia. When everyone has taken a crack at it, the original author can polish and post the final version.

Posting Multiple Obits

Alternatively, two or more separate obits can be posted back to back. This trend takes advantage of the unlimited space available in an online platform. It also lets friends, family, and colleagues portray the obituee in his various roles—father, teacher, coach, friend, volunteer, and so on.

The people of Iceland have a charming tradition of writing letter-style obituaries in which the obituarist speaks directly to the obituee. This is called "writing after" the deceased person. You might say, for instance, that Kolka Bjarnason (both common names in Iceland, believe it or not) had eight obituaries written after her.

The most unusual feature of this tradition is that each letter to the dead is not *the* obituary, but *an* obituary—that is, one of many. Major newspapers in Iceland publish these multiple obits free of charge.

In the United States and elsewhere, sympathetic comments on memorial pages and online obits echo the Icelandic tradition of writing after the dead. For example, fellow officers and citizens might post remembrances on the memorial site for a police officer killed in the line of duty. Such comments are often lengthy and directed toward the deceased. It's like speaking at the graveside, says author Erinn Staley, except that "this new medium [may] over time facilitate community among the living in a way that many other rituals surrounding death do not."[6]

When John "Jack" Sullivan died in 2012, each of his three children wrote a remembrance of him. These affectionate pieces, which are among my favorites, have a sincerity and warmth that's missing in many traditional obits. It's likely they were used as eulogies. Adapting a eulogy into an obit or vice versa is perfectly fine. No need to reinvent the wheel.

SHOULD YOU WRITE YOUR OWN OBITUARY?

Nothing calls you to account like trying to describe your unique contribution to humanity in 1,300 words or less. "[By doing] what you're doing every day, you're writing your own obituary," says Heather Lende, a professional obituarist and hospice volunteer.[7] But hey, no pressure…

Is it a good idea to write your own obit—your autobituary? Many newspaper editors have dismissed this "unhealthy indulgence" as garbage—literally and figuratively. Self-penned obits, said the late Anthony Howard, former obituaries editor for *The Times* of London, "invariably and unfailingly amount to anthems of self-praise." They go "straight into the WPB [waste-paper basket]."[8] Nevertheless, many a reporter has been known to write his or her own send-off.[9] Let's look at the pros and cons.

Downside of Writing an Autobituary

When Stephen Lock was the obituaries editor for the prestigious *British Medical Journal,* he was initially open to publishing autobituaries within the journal's pages. He later came to side with the newspaper editors. Selfie obits, he discovered, tend to defend the author's choices, excuse bad behavior, and swoon over modest accomplishments. "Too often, the attempt turns out to be a self justification or an apologia," he wrote in 1995.[10]

Having written my own obituary in preparation for this book, I can vouch for how hard it is to pull off without falling into the aforementioned traps. Another sticky issue is deciding which colleagues and friends and family members to mention. It's hard not to channel Sally Field's Oscar acceptance speech: "And I'd like to thank Mrs. Dickerson for teaching me how to diagram sentences…"

The exercise is like drawing up a list of wedding guests: How can you thank Mrs. Dickerson without mentioning your rabbi, your barista, and the guy who did your last oil change? And after everything you put your parents through as a teenager, are you really going to devote as much space to your love of bedazzling as you do to your childhood? You get the idea.

Appraising your own achievements in an obituary is as humiliating as writing your own performance review at work, minus the chance to do better next year. In your effort to avoid sounding defensive or arrogant or glib, you might undersell yourself. If your daughter or a lifelong friend were to write your obit, she might be kinder and more generous in her praise than you are to yourself.

Unfortunately, says Stephen Hancocks in an editorial for the *British Dental Journal,* we rarely have the advantage of knowing what people say about us in our obituary.[11] If we did, though, we might be flattered rather than disappointed.

Upside of Writing an Autobituary

Appraising your own lifetime performance can be a profound experience. Scientist and writer Oliver Sacks lived 6 months after learning he was terminally ill. "Over the last few days," he wrote in the *New York Times,* "I have been able to see my life as from a great altitude, as a sort of landscape, and with a deepening sense of the connection of all of its parts."

Writing your obit is a kind gesture that relieves your grieving family of a burden. Working with your loved ones to prepare it, especially if you're building a virtual memorial, is a wonderful way to reminisce and draw closer—maybe even heal old wounds—as the end of life draws near.

Penning an autobituary also keeps you from joining the nameless ranks of those who were "dearly loved" and will be "greatly missed." If you leave the task to someone else, your passing may be marked with only a nondescript death notice stating the facts of your demise couched in a few sappy clichés.

It's true that an autobituary can become a raft from which to launch excuses and float belated apologies. Some of us, though, welcome the chance to admit our mistakes or, if you're like this fellow, confess to larceny and one really ballsy lie:

> As it turns out, I AM the guy who stole the safe from the Motor View Drive Inn back in June, 1971…Also, I really am NOT a PhD…I only had about 3 years of college credit…For all of the Electronic Engineers I have worked with, I'm sorry. –*Autobituary, Val Patterson (1953–2012)*

These days, each of us has a real life and an optimized digital persona populated by Instagram pics, blog entries, pinboards, tweets, Facebook posts, and other digital breadcrumbs. This curated presence excludes the unbecoming and unpleasant. Bad bosses, catfights, sleep deprivation, sibling rivalry, muffin tops, and credit card debt are edged out by duckface, studio lighting, beachy hair, puppies, positive reinforcement, and the milk of human kindness.

Why stop now? An autobituary coalesces those virtual moments into a final, kaleidoscopic selfie. "I work too hard in this life to be misunderstood after death," explains one self-obituarist.[12] "It takes guts to put [your story] on paper and let other people read it," says another.[13] In that spirit, here's mine:

> I'm not a finisher. My past is a scrap heap of unlearned languages, partially built websites, halfhearted DIY attempts, unentered 5K races, instruments I can't play, and at least one ill-advised marriage—but who's counting? I did, at least, stick to my plan of going to college, and by age 23 I had earned a master's degree. I worked at Saint Louis University by day and taught English comp classes for a few semesters in the evenings before landing a job in the production department of a medical textbook company.
>
> The publishing house was a refuge for some odd ducks. One was a timid savant named George, who spoke to me only once,

when I spilled popcorn on the staircase. Without missing a beat, he scooped up a handful of kernels and began popping them into his mouth, explaining that exposing oneself to random microbes was good for the ol' immune system.

I shared a cubicle partition with a quirky character named Carl, a loner who studied Native American dialects in his free time. Carl was so tightfisted that for lunch he'd sometimes bring a salad of dandelion greens, lamb's quarters, and mushrooms harvested from the lawn of his suburban home.

We copyeditors had in common a deep respect for language. "If you take hyphens seriously, you will surely go mad," declares the *Oxford Style Manual.* Oh, how we'd quarrel over hyphenation and capitalization! Back then we did everything old school (or is it old-school?), with pica poles, mechanical pencils, Scotch tape, and scissors. We soon began using PCs, initiating the inevitable transition to electronic publishing, and to an industry with little tolerance for methodical misfits like George and Carl.

I felt at home among those introverts and fussbudgets. A cranky, dogmatic English teacher named Mrs. Dickerson had indoctrinated me early in the militant craft of sentence diagramming. As a kid, I'd been most at ease in the company of Jo March, Cherry Ames, and Templeton the rat.

With a boyish haircut and lenses thicker than auto glass, I looked the part of the bashful bookworm. Until I had my teeth fixed, Freddie Mercury had nothin' on me. I had blemishes that might as well have been smallpox, as far as I was concerned. "You'll be a butterfly someday," my mother assured me, based on zero evidence. My self-consciousness was compounded by being "the new girl" as my military family shuffled from state to state—South Carolina, Texas, Alabama, California, Maryland, Illinois, Florida.

I was never a butterfly, but I became a passable moth. By the time my then-boyfriend Brian decided to go ahead and marry me already, we'd been dating 8 years and I was in my late 30s. My youthful desire to have children of my own had come and gone, but I did gain a terrific stepson, Christopher.

It was my nature to fret over everything—cash flow, crepey skin, cockroaches, landfills, the collapse of democracy, tire pressure, password security…and that's just off the top of my head. I counted my blessings and dreaded losing them at the same time. My fears were borne out now and then, but fractures healed, disks were replaced, retinas repaired. Friendships sometimes proved harder to mend.

I had plenty of reason to feel fulfilled. There were the big things, of course. My mother was healthy. My work was gratifying. I had married a fastidious, dependable Felix Unger type with the glib charm and charisma of a Sam Malone. But I rarely took for granted even the most humdrum amenities—hot baths, clean sheets, insecticide, central heating, foaming hand soap.

Most of the half-baked ideas and false starts on the slag pile I leave behind are where they belong. But I did save one lump from the rubble: a book on modern obituary writing. I hope it inspired readers to appreciate their loved ones' unique stories and to tell them with warmth, wit, and a whiff of *chutzpah*.

Best Practices for Writing Your Own Send-Off

These days, more and more people are preparing autobituaries or end-of-life memorials. They've lived on their own terms, and they want to die that way, too. "I don't want anyone to ever have to guess who I was or what I accomplished," explains one woman.[14] See Chapter 8 for more on life review sites.

If you do begin an autobituary, finish it! At any moment, the ferry might make an unscheduled departure with you aboard. You know that, or you wouldn't be writing your obituary in the first place. If you leave the document incomplete, your family may find and publish it that way. Until it's finished, label your draft something like this:

> This obituary, last updated in June 2017, is a work in progress. If I should achieve room temperature before completing it, please do not post or publish it [or, depending on your wishes, "please finish it and post it for me"]. –Chris P. Bacon, Des Moines, Iowa, 15 August 2018

If your writing is intended to be a private memoir, not an autobituary, be sure to label it to that effect. I ran across one such piece peppered with notes to self that the writer never had a chance to follow up on, such as "Dad found work at the Kingsville Do-nut House on Main/Broadway?" This document was published in lieu of an obituary. It ends abruptly with an indelicate comment about some friends that probably wasn't intended for public consumption: "They are up to their eyeballs in debt."

Some would-be autobituarists hesitate because they question whether their story is worth telling. "An obituary is a testament to a life that has been lived," said the late obituary columnist Tom Vartabedian. "Don't think your life is any less significant than any other."[15]

Your autobituary will never be posted, of course, if no one knows it exists. Once it's finished, label the piece with its purpose, your name, and the date and place of completion:

> –Autobituary by Chris P. Bacon, Des Moines, Iowa, 10 October 2018

Then what? Well, posting the obit yourself is an option. An autobituary can be part of a larger project—an end-of-life review aimed at preserving stories and memories for your loved ones. After your death, the site can serve as your virtual memorial.

Several apps are designed to store your autobituary, your will, and other important documents "forever" (see Chapter 8 for details). Upon your death, the app makes the documents available to one or more trustees you designate in advance. Forever ends, though, if the app's investors pull the plug. It'll take time for the competition to shake out in this crowded space. Be sure to choose an app that has solid financial backing and a broad customer base. As a backup, consider giving a hard copy of your obituary and other papers to your attorney, if you have one, or to a family member or trusted friend.

If that archaic process is too much of a hassle, store your obit and important documents in the cloud—Dropbox, iCloud, Google Drive, or a similar storage service. Designate a legacy contact to access the files after your death.

If you'd like a particular family member or friend to add an afterword to your selfie, leave instructions for him or her. After all, you don't know how your own story will end. Once your package has been wrapped, someone else must put a bow on it.

WHOSE PERSPECTIVE WILL YOU REPRESENT?

When you write an obituary for a loved one, members of your family may not like what you say or how you say it. But trying to appease everyone is like putting too many spices into your dry rub: none of the flavors will shine. Decide whether you owe your loyalty to the obituee, to yourself, or to some other person or group, such as future generations. Then write with that audience in mind.

You'll also need to choose a point of view (POV)—a so-called "narrative voice"—remember that from ninth-grade English? The first-, second-, or third-person POV indicates that the subject (the obituee) is speaking, being spoken to, or being spoken about, respectively. Let's say the deceased is Frieda Kalt:

First Person

If Mrs. Kalt had written her own obituary, she'd probably use a first-person POV. In this voice, Mrs. Kalt herself is the speaker ("My spätzle won a blue ribbon at the 1973 Polk County German-American Heritage Fest"). The pronouns *I, me, my,* and *mine* in the singular and *we, us, our,* and *ours* in the plural indicate the first-person POV.

Second Person

Let's say Mrs. Kalt's daughter, Greta, writes an obit in the second person. In this voice, the obituee is being spoken *to:* "I'll think of you every time I make a batch of spätzle," Greta might say. Although that sentence begins with "I," it addresses Mrs. Kalt directly ("you"). The pronouns *you, your,* and *yours* indicate the second person. This POV focuses equally on the speaker's loss and the obituee's life. Use restraint with this POV, though, or it can sound schlocky.

Third Person

A third-person narrative tells the story from an objective, detached perspective in which the obituee is being spoken *about.* This POV uses the pronouns *he, she, it, his, hers, him, her,* and *its* in the singular and *they, them, their,* and *theirs* in the plural. A third-person obit might report that "every year during deer season,

Frieda made grilled venison with hazelnut spätzle and cider-poached pears." The third-person voice places greater emphasis on the obituee than on the speaker:

> John made numerous and wide-ranging contributions to experimental psychology and visual science. *–John Krauskopf (1928–2016)*

Some selfie obits mimic this style—that is, they're written by the obituee as if he or she were writing about someone else. Using the third person lets you to say nice things about yourself without coming off as a windbag. This POV can sound barmy, though, if readers know who actually wrote the piece. A talented self-obituarist can exploit this awkwardness for comic effect:

> Kevin J. McGroarty, 53, of West Pittston, died Tuesday, July 22, 2014, after battling a long fight with mediocrity. *–Autobituary, Kevin J. McGroarty (1960–2014)*

Your POV can influence your choices about tone, content, and even platform. Experiment to see what works for you. I started out writing my obit in the third person: "Until Melissa had her teeth fixed…" It didn't feel right, so I switched to the first person, which seems more natural.

Don't worry if your point of view alternates a bit. For example, some obits are written in the third person throughout, but conclude with a message to the deceased ("We'll miss you. Give Mom a hug and a kiss from us!") or to mourners ("We're grateful for the outpouring of sympathy we've received from those who loved Carter as much as we did").

WHO WILL HANDLE THE TECH SIDE?

If you plan to post more than a photo or two with the tribute you're putting together, you'll need to know something about technology—or work with someone who does.

If your skills are rusty and there's a computer nerd in your family, why not combine your strengths? One of you can write the obit and supply video narration, photo captions, and so on.

The other can choose a memorial platform and then digitize, edit, and upload your images, video, audio clips, and music. He or she can also share the finished memorial on social media.

HOW LONG WILL THE OBITUARY BE?

A Rule of Thumb

Most tributes appear with only a single photo, or perhaps with a slide show or photo gallery. But a growing proportion of obituaries serve as the anchor for a more extensive virtual memorial (also known as a "digital memorial"). There are no hard-and-fast limits in either case, but 600–1,200 words in length is a good rule of thumb. To get some idea of how long that is in print, see the 1,000-word obituary I wrote in advance for my mother (Chapter 6). My autobituary, which appears earlier in this chapter, is a bit shorter, coming in at less than 800 words.

How Long Is Too Long?

In an online tribute, space is unlimited. But even the cleverest obituary can be too long. A good obit writer, says author Marilyn Johnson, can "capture a person with economy and grace."[16]

Family members and self-obituarists have a tough time with the "economy" part of the equation. Our instinct is to turn the obit into a biographical sketch or memoir. In any life, the narrative arc—that is, the scope of the story—naturally moves from cradle to grave. But that doesn't mean you must present your obituary or life story in that order, or that you have to cover everything that happened in the middle. Instead, select details and brief stories that capture the obituee's essence and offer a snapshot of his or her world. You might decide to skip the obituee's childhood years, for example, or omit the heartbreak of her dementia.

How Short Is Too Short?

Sometimes what you don't say is more telling than what you do. I once worked with an author whose wife had died shortly before the book went to press. He told me pointedly that there would be no dedication for that edition. The next edition was dedicated to his dogs.

If you've cobbled together less than 500 words and you're not trying to make a statement in saying so little, you probably need to flesh out your portrait with additional detail. Review the checklist at the end of Chapter 4 for ideas.

WHAT TONE WILL YOU USE?

Thomas Mallon wrote the foreword for a collection of pieces by celebrated *New York Times* obituary writer Robert McG. Thomas Jr. Mr. Mallon notes that Mr. Thomas "could be a New Orleans jazz band or a hushed friar as occasion demanded."[17] In other words, Mr. Thomas let the obituee and the story of his or her life dictate the tone of his tribute.

Begin thinking about your obituee's life and personality, the circumstances of his or her death, and your audience (see the discussion of perspective earlier in this chapter). The right tone will follow from those considerations. For example, if your obituee was elderly—the product of a cherished bygone era— your tribute may have a nostalgic bent. Nostalgia is the point at which emotion and memory intersect. It's "delicate but potent," says Don Draper in *Mad Men*. "It's a twinge in your heart far more powerful than memory alone."

If your obituee was a bon vivant—an adventurer or a gourmand, say—your tone might be lighthearted as you toast a life well lived. If he or she was more straightlaced, you can dial it down a notch or two. For example, you might write an understated tribute for a judge or scientist, or for someone with a brilliant military record or other distinguished achievements. But for heaven's sake, don't be a crepehanger. Respectful doesn't mean dull. Likewise, words of consolation are in order when the obituee's death was untimely, but some tasteful humor brings needed levity to the situation.

WHERE WILL YOU POST THE OBIT OR MEMORIAL?

You need not commit to a platform at this stage, but begin thinking about it, since the website, app, or virtual memorial you choose will affect your content and media selections. A tribute posted to website of your husband's army regiment, for example, would say something different from one posted for family and friends. It would also feature different photos, videos, and music.

Look for a memorial with brisk, well-moderated site traffic—it's likely to stick around for the long term. The platform should be affordable, attractive, and easy to navigate. It should offer flexible, interactive features. (See Chapter 8 for a detailed discussion of virtual memorial options and features.) You don't necessarily have to post on just one site. You might dash off a quick text-centric obit for the army regiment, for instance, but take your time building a more media-centric tribute in another venue.

NEXT STEPS

By now, you've made some decisions about authorship, collaboration, audience, length, and tone. You've begun to investigate where you'll house your main tribute and any variations of it. Chapter 4 will help you collect information about your obituee's life. (If you know him or her well, this task will be more a sorting exercise than a gathering process.) Then you'll organize that information into a narrative that celebrates the obituee's individuality, applauds his or her achievements and gifts, and stands as a memorial to his life and times. "If one does not die well," said Filipino leader José Rizal, "a good opportunity is lost and will not present itself again."

Chapter 4

JUST THE QUIRKS, MA'AM
Collecting Your Memories

Thank goodness for Bart Simpson, Buzzfeed, and the Kardashians, who have collectively made it okay not to be so mad-stodgy all the time. Oh, don't get me wrong. Death is serious. It's wrenching to lose someone you love even when it was time, let alone watch someone die too soon. But do you want to mark the end of your loved one's joyful life by memorializing your own sorrow? Instead, use the power of language and technology to capture his or her spirit.

Jot some notes as you read this chapter and your memories bubble to the surface (trust me—they will). You might want to create a sort of word cloud composed of things, people, places, sounds, scents, foods, song lyrics—anything that reminds you of the obituee.

A mindmap or brainstorming app can help you sort through this ragbag of memories. Open-source (free) mind-mapping apps such as FreeMind let you tag your ideas with emoji, dates, color-coded flags, or icons (such as "To be refined" or "To be discussed"). Niftier apps, such as MindNode, are available for about thirty bucks at the high end. They have snazzier user interfaces, easier navigation, and better functionality, such as drag-and-drop tools. You can also import images or link websites and documents within these apps.

Your word cloud or mindmap doesn't have to make sense to anyone but you. When I began thinking about my mom's pre-need obit (see Chapter 6), here's what came to mind:

- Lipstick and Shalimar
- Hostess cupcakes
- Toni home perms
- Dried frogs
- Gardening
- Boating
- Road trips
- Museums & art
- Sequins
- Dinner party hostess
- Rat experiment
- 22 homes
- Top salesperson
- Grandson
- Phone calls
- Cleaning

At this stage, don't worry about spelling or sequence or grammatical parallelism. (And if you don't remember what grammatical parallelism is, be grateful that you can't be tormented by it.) Just get the thoughts out of your head and onto the screen or page. Later you'll make connections among them and illustrate them with quotations, physical descriptions, sensory impressions, and other elements that give the writing greater specificity. You'll also end up scrapping the items that don't fit.

This process is a lot like cooking. To prepare a good dish, a chef assembles his equipment, utensils, and ingredients—the *mise en pláce* ("everything in place")—before ever lighting a burner. Likewise, you're gathering specific details to draw on as you write (see Chapter 5 for more on writing a draft).

We do need to jump ahead for a moment, though. After all, a chef must know what dish he'll be cooking before he sources his ingredients. So let's talk about the makings of a memorable obituary before we go to market.

THE DIFFERENCE BETWEEN TELLING AND SHOWING

"Don't tell me the moon is shining," said playwright Anton Chekhov. "Show me the glint of light on broken glass." Whether you're a poet or a cub reporter, the principle is the same: a good writer doesn't tell—she shows. In that spirit, there's no need for me to explain what I mean. See for yourself:

> **Telling:** He was a hard worker and achieved his highest potential in everything he did.
> **Showing:** After retirement from CGS [California Geological Survey] in 1994, he was back in the San Francisco office the next working day. His devotion to geology kept him coming back for the next nine years. *–Earl William Hart (1927–2016)*

> **Telling:** She loved animals.
> **Showing:** When one [of her cats] died, the word would go out in cat circles and a new stray would appear at the back door to take up residence. *–Constance Marlatt Huested Allen (1940–2016)*

> **Telling:** He was an accomplished skier.
> **Showing:** A three-year stint in the Army provided Jim a chance to use his skiing prowess, [and] he won first prize in a downhill/slalom and cross-country race in 1954 in Berchtesgaden, Germany. *–James Whitehead Glover (1933–2010)*

> **Telling:** [He] liked to sing and perform.
> **Showing:** Phil had a true, clear tenor voice…He was very proud of nailing the high "F" in "There is Nothing like a Dame" in Evergreen Chorale's production of South Pacific. *–Philip Riedesel (1935–2015)*

> **Telling:** She was careful with her money.
> **Showing:** To the end she was meticulous in balancing the checkbook and could spend whatever time it took (sometimes hours) to reconcile down to the penny. *–Hazel Maurine Roggy (1923–2016)*

Telling: Everyone will remember her amazing meals and fun conversations in her always spotless kitchen.

Showing: Jack enjoyed…hosting family holiday gatherings and large dinner parties. Guests invariably commented on his specially-made, alphabetically-organized 75-jar spice rack hanging prominently in the kitchen, which wittily ended with a jar labeled "Waiting for Godot." *–John W. Aber Jr. (~1938–2015)*

Of course, it's fine to tell first and *then* show. That's a tidy way of organizing related points or transitioning to a new idea. The first sentence gives a wide shot of the topic, and the remaining sentences bring it into sharper focus:

> Goldie was a very hard worker. At age thirteen he got his first job mowing lawns with a push mower. He made one dollar for every front yard he mowed and one dollar for every back yard as well. He then started delivering the Seattle [Post-Intelligencer] and the Seattle Star on a bicycle at 5:00 am every morning…He earned his first car, a 1931 Chevrolet, by digging out his neighbor's basement with a pick and shovel. *–Goldwyn O. "Goldie" Gjerding (1931–2014)*

Has the obituarist persuaded you that Goldie worked his butt off? Yeah…me, too. But the paragraph's topic sentence is not what convinced us—it was all the delicious detail that followed.

GATHERING DETAILS

Writers resort to telling, rather than showing, when they don't have enough information. That means you'll have to collect lots of details about your obituee. Much of this information will end up in the compost bin, but the more you have to start with, the easier your task will be. Use a recording app or take notes as you talk to people. Trust but verify. Here are some other tips:

- If possible, interview the would-be obituee himself before his daily subscription is canceled.
- Talk to the obituee's family, friends, colleagues, pastor, golfing buddies, or supper-club partners.
- If your obituee owned a business, ask employees and long-time customers to share their favorite memories.

- If he or she frequented a local pub or diner, talk to other regulars, as well as the barkeep and servers.
- If you interview only one person, make it the obituee's hairstylist. You're apt to learn more from him or her than from anyone else.
- Check the bookshelf in the obituee's home. Is it filled with presidential biographies? Harry Potter books? Graphic novels? What do these choices tell you?
- Check the obituee's Amazon wish list and Goodreads posts for clues, too. What do her choices and comments say about her interests and personality?
- Look at your obituee's Facebook page, Instagram pics, pinboards, tweets, Reddit posts, and other social media.

It's a bad idea, though, to comb through your obituee's email, chat logs, and so on. Even in death, people have a right to privacy. You might find out something you can't unknow. Besides, it would be a little creepy, right?

In the next few sections, we'll go over specific details that will spice up your tribute.

Nicknames

Explaining the origin of a nickname is an easy way to liven up an obit. Nicknames often illustrate a character trait ("Boss," "Storm") or physical feature ("Greyhound," "Rughead," "Bigfoot"). Some reflect a hobby, job, or skill ("Inspector Gadget," "Mr. Artichoke"):

> Her 15 minutes of fame came at WHO Radio, where listeners of the Van and Connie Show knew her as Fluffy Croissant (for her bouffant hairdo and for the many delicious baked goods she brought to the station). —*Violet Marie Casady (1924–2013)*

> [S]he used to wade out and catch minnows in her apron to use as fishing bait. In fact, one of her uncles used to call her his "Little Brown Duck" because her skin was tan from being outside so much, and she could always be found wading along the banks of the waterfront. —*Corinne Alice Flukinger (1930–2014)*

40

As a small girl, her mom used to call her "Velcro" because she couldn't move or go anywhere without DeeDee clinging to her. *—Deandra "DeeDee" Charisse Fegurgur (1992–2016)*

He earned the nickname "Barney"...after a few minor mishaps similar to Barney Fife's. [He] shot off the police chief's doorknob with a supposedly unloaded service revolver...The Andy Griffith Show reruns were then known as Officer Butler's training tapes. *—William Francis "Barney" Butler (1939–2014)*

Formative Experiences and Defining Traits

Luck

Even the most self-disciplined person is shaped by forces beyond his or her control. Illness, accidents, and tattoo hangovers happen. So do happy coincidences and strokes of good luck. What were the "sliding door" events in your obituee's life? What kind of person did he or she become as a result?

During this period [of childhood illness], her father read to her literary classics and she also entertained herself with coloring books, creating paper cut-outs and browsing through dance magazines. *—Helen King Boyer (1919–2012)*

Growing up in the Great Depression, Wilma learned lessons in frugality that she would carry throughout her life. No food was wasted in the Zummak household; still-wearable shoes got cardboard inserts when the soles became worn; and scraps of paper were folded and saved to be used again. *—Wilma Althea "Willie" (Zummak) Anderson (1918–2016)*

[He] entered WW II in 1944 as a 1st Lieutenant in the 4454th Quartermaster Service Company. He was put in command of a unit of black enlisted men. That experience changed his life, upsetting the prejudices of what had been a sheltered existence, and started Jim on a life-long course of progressive liberalism and commitment to social justice. *—James E. Boman (1922–2015)*

In 2003 he and Sharon visited Africa on a photo safari and the experience changed their lives. Bill wrote and published a book, illustrated with his photographs, entitled *The Call of Africa*, and donated all proceeds to Heifer International. *–Joel William "Bill" Allgood, M.D. (1936–2014)*

Family Roles

What was your obituee's function within the family ecosystem? Was he the patriarch? The comedian? The black sheep? Explain.

> Her task [of caring for her siblings after their mother's premature death] was compounded when little brother Ed fell from a school slide and hit his head on the bricks. The children took him home in their wagon to heal. No doctor was called, and months later Ed developed seizures and was thereafter handicapped. *–Anne Margaret Angel (1912–2013)*

> He was the family counselor, social director, private investigator (snitch), Santa Claus, menu consultant (meat loaf, Zack?), and fashion critic (you need a haircut). *–Rodney Jones (1957–2010)*

> Bill was smart, with a kopf for figures, but Fay was smarter. She ran their family, home, and finances, with love, firmness, and an economy learned in the Depression. Like everything Florence did, she managed everything competently and with no fuss. *–Florence Spatrick (1917–2014)*

Family Legends

Every family has a story that's been repeated and exaggerated over the years. It might not be 100% true, but you can be sure it's colorful. Ask family and friends to share tales like these:

> One of the stories she loved to tell about her time [as a child] in France was when, as a three year old, she comforted her au pair during a thunderstorm. The au pair hid in a closet and little Gloria stood at the door saying *"Ne pas peur, Marcelle. Je suis ici."* *–Gloria (Bedikian) Ayvazian (1923–2015)*

> Family legend has it that Bethany sang before she talked and was often found crooning the song "Blue Velvet" in her crib. *–Bethany Kay Bereman (1961–2011)*

The doctor had just laid the stillborn infant, wrapped in a blanket, onto the table, and he and the others worked feverishly over the mother to save her life. It had been a difficult birth and just as they decided that the mother was going to make it, they heard a tiny sound coming from the direction of the table. Quickly the doctor rushed to the small bundle and found that the infant was alive! –*Bud Arvin Brakey (1923–2016)*

[While closing her stepfather's soda fountain one night], a pair of men burst in brandishing pistols and demanded that she empty the till…There was only five dollars in the register, and that didn't satisfy the robbers. She coolly [made up a story to explain the missing cash, which she'd concealed]…Then the men took the five dollars and cleared out… –*Mary Elizabeth (Springman) Lively (1911–2016)*

"How We Met" Stories

If the box-office success of *The Notebook* is any indication, we're suckers for random acts of romance like these:

[T]hey met on a blind date. She was standing on the front porch wearing a blue dress, eating a biscuit. She got in the front seat and never left. –*Wilfred "Bub" Atwood (1918–2010)*

Evelyn and Holly met under the mirrored globe at the Electric Park Ballroom in Waterloo. –*Evelyn Laurel (Luth) Borland (1924–2015)*

They met while handing out sack lunches to the homeless as part of the Cathedral's Good Samaritan program. –*Christopher Robert Blodgett (1963–2013)*

Characteristic Phrases or Advice

Ask friends, family, and acquaintances to recall words or phrases they associate with the obituee:

And he always pushed his kids to try new things. His favorite motivating statement was to tell them, "It'll put hair on your chest!" –*Gregory Lewis Richards (1961–2012)*

Whenever they would arrive home, James would ask Amalia to check the answering machine and when there were no messages, he would say "Nobody loves me, everybody hates me, I guess I'll go eat worms; big fat juicy ones, little short slimy ones, any old kind that'll squirm." *–James V. Jones Sr. (1912–2015)*

If asked how he was doing, he'd always say, "I'm hanging in there like a rusty fish hook." *–William R. Porter Jr. (1935–2013)*

Grammy…left her loved ones with many lessons: Decorate and talk to your plants. Work your core. Dance even if you're in a chair. Take photos and star in them, too. "Whatever" is the perfect response for most scenarios. Don't pass up a chance to go to Target or to see the Weiner Mobile. *–Doris Puckett (1918–2014)*

Typical Behavior

My mother says I'll be late to my own funeral. I'm also klutzy and scatterbrained. Traits like these are baked in. On my very first report card, the teacher wrote "Easily distracted." What do people remember about your obituee's habits and behavior?

[He] called himself a gerbil…and with an engineer's discipline, kept track of just how many times (numbering into the thousands) he went around that track. *–Philip Riedesel (1935–2015)*

He spent hours listening to music in his family's living room, feet propped up the stereo console, a cigarette burning in one hand and a can of Coke always nearby. *–Philip F. Welsh Jr. (1948–2014)*

Good Deeds

Seems like the people who do the most good are the least likely to toot their own horns. Here's your chance to do it for them:

In all, due to Herman and Miriam's efforts, over 80 relatives were saved from certain death in the concentration camps of occupied Europe. Of the Davidovits clan, over 207 who chose to remain were exterminated in Auschwitz and other camps. It is through this prism that Dad developed his commitment to family that defined virtually every aspect of his life. *–Leon Davis (1918–2013)*

He would go to different orchards and pick up pecans to make pralines, turtles and peanut brittle [and] then deliver them to different wards at hospitals, nursing homes, co-workers family and friends. –*Elmer Russell Garmer (1923–2016)*

Physical Characteristics

Our obsession with physical appearance can be pretty shallow. It's why we take selfies and comb through our friends' timelines and boards. It's why we swipe left or right on Grindr. But human survival depends on our ability to distinguish familiar faces from unknown people who may pose a threat. Studies show that this ability to recognize others through "visual, auditory and linguistic channels" is hard-wired into our brains.[1] Visual recognition is the most important of these channels.

If you're writing your own obit, how do people recognize *you?* Is it your beer belly, your schnozz, your billboard brow? Give readers enough detail to form a mental picture:

Mom grew into a stunning beautiful young woman…with long dark hair, ivory skin, green eyes and a signature gap in her two front teeth, just like the actress Lauren Hutton. –*Geraldine Anna Conrad (1929–2016)*

Many San Angelo residents will remember Joy as the K-Mart lady with the birthmark at the service desk where she worked for 23 years. –*Millie Joy Dickson Meurer (1930–2013)*

John graduated with a Bachelor of Arts from the University of California Santa Barbara, a proud brother of Sigma Chi Fraternity, and perhaps the only red-headed, freckled surfer on the beach. –*John Robert Bothwell II (1951–2016)*

Clothing

Our clothing choices are so predictable that we're surprised when a collar man breaks character and wears a Henley, say, or when a Dickies-and–ball cap kind of guy rocks a fedora. Was your obituee the velour track suit type, or did she favor A-line dresses and pencil skirts?

Luis always said his rainbow suspenders, which he wore daily, represented all the colors and ethnicities of the planet. *–Luis Ellicott Yglesias (1936–2014)*

He was the closest thing that Fayetteville ever saw to a true drug store cowboy, preferring leather fringe to three piece suits. *–Ronald E. Bumpass (1948–2014)*

It is no surprise that he asked to be cremated in Taz pajamas, with wooly slippers and a rugby ball under his arm. *–Michael Joseph Ireland (1961–2016)*

After graduation and the start of WWII, our mother joined the war effort and moved to Long Beach, California to work at Douglas Aircraft Company as a riveter. She could have easily been Rockwell's model for "Rosie the Riveter" with her tied up red hair, coveralls and saddle shoes. *–Wilma J. Edwards (1921–2016)*

Hair and Makeup

Some of us change hairstyles every few months. Others cling to a signature look—I'm talking to you, Anna Wintour. Either way, supplying those details adds texture to your portrait:

Freddy was notorious for always having the latest hairstyle, from congolene like James Brown, to big curls like Barry White, to a Jeri curl, afro and mohawk! *–Frederick Douglas Brown (1939–2014)*

Imbued with a flair for the dramatic, C was distinguished by her self-styled hairdo, which featured not only a broad, bisecting streak of white, but also a unilateral, wind-swept prominence. Oh, my. *–Charmian Akins (1922–2015)*

We all laughed about how she would dress in all white, put on her false eyelashes, go fishing, and never get dirty. *–Lucille Collins Harvey (1935–2013)*

Body Language

Could you identify your spouse or child on camera if her face were pixelated? Probably so—you know how he or she walks

and stands, how she cocks her head. Now picture your obituee.
Read his body language, and tell the reader what you see:

> He then spent decades walking the streets of Louisville, especially
> up and down Bardstown Road in the Highlands, where many
> people recognized him for the distinctive way he churned his arm
> as he walked. *–William Rice (1937–2016)*

> [I]f you said or did anything that rubbed her the wrong way she
> would tilt her head [and]…stare at you with a slight frown.
> *–Mother Josephine (Franklin) Davis (1926-2011)*

> Joanne spent many hours crafting miniature doll clothes for her
> children. (She didn't much enjoy sewing Barbie clothes, which
> caused her to purse her lips, furrow her brow, and growl at her
> sewing machine.) She would always present the results with great
> pride and triumph. *–Joanne Marie Knittle (1945–2014)*

> I met Theda while serving as activity director at Valley Springs.
> We dubbed her the "door keeper" as she sat by the front door and
> would stand with her back to the glass so the sunshine could warm
> her. *–Guest book entry for Theda Leonard (1917–2005)*

Other Sensory Impressions

Voice and Speech Patterns

Decades after a loved one dies, we can still hear his or her voice
in our mind's ear. Conjuring up an obituee's voice for the reader,
of course, is as difficult as describing a fragrance. If you have
audio clips—or video clips with sound—problem solved. If not,
a general description still helps round out your portrait. How did
the obituee "sound" in writing?

> He texted like Tarzan… "Hi Hill, how you? Me good. Cold here.
> Wood stove going." *–Peter Elliott Huckel (1939–2016)*

Was the obituee soft-spoken or sharp-tongued? Was her accent
lilting and aristocratic or twangy and nasal? Her voice reedy or
resonant? Her laugh a cackle or a chortle, a snicker or a snort?

Effervescent and full of spunk until the very end, Cookie would routinely remark to the curious bystander who would ask "Are you from New York…", commenting on her trademark raspy and stentorian North East accent, "No", she would boast, "I'm from New Jersey." –*Natalie Ann "Cookie" Iorio (1933–2017)*

She talked like a New Orleanian: her accent was so strong that someone once asked if she came with an interpreter. –*Mary Margaret Brazier (1956–2016)*

Scents or Odors

In the human brain, the sense of smell is closely tied to memory. In fact, scents and odors deliver more of an emotional gut-punch than verbally or visually evoked memories because they take us back further.[2] The scent of watermelon or petunias or clover can trigger memories going back to early childhood. My only memory of my great-grandfather Hye, for example, is the smell of the butterscotch candies he kept in his pocket.

As you collect information and jot down your own memories of your obituee, don't neglect the sense of smell. Ask friends and family who knew your obituee what scents or aromas they associate with him or her:

Aldo was also a closet master baker. He baked dozens upon dozens of exquisite Italian cookies to share with friends and family at Christmas. The smell of biscotti and chess pies will forever remind us of his ability to bring people together with laughter in the kitchen. –*Aldo Gino Antongiovanni (1926–2013)*

The house smelled like a gym for years while she laundered sporting uniforms and cheerleading outfits. –*Barbara Kegel (1923-2015)*

The scent of sawdust, and the audible grinding of tools, were commonplace in his home. –*Henry Ellis "Harry Bodine II (1941–2017)*

Touch and Texture

The sense of touch is so omnipresent that it's easy to forget. As you parse the nuances of your obituee's life, think about consistency, temperature, and texture: damp, oily, squishy, spiky, brittle, frosty, crisp, chapped, chalky, crusty, slick, muddy, spongy, dense, and so on:

> The feel, texture and weight of books were a favorite of Rae's. When e-readers became available she rapidly converted but always missed a "real" book. *–Rae Jeannette Howe (1956–2016)*

> Her favorite summer activities were hiking and camping where she would roast marshmallows and (yes, with sticky hands) find ways to create art with natural, found materials in the forest. *–Teah Penninah Mantzke (2003–2013)*

> Susan's brightly colored, glittery & hairy crocheted hats were sold at many crafts fairs locally. They were owned and envied by many. *–Susan Gayle Anderson (1946–2016)*

> Flora's tiny hands first reached to hold her mother's, Rosa Lee Warren's finger on November 15, 1923. Those same tiny hands would hold tightly to the calloused farmer hands of her father, William Alonzo Weathers. *–Flora Weathers Clark (1923–2013)*

Flavor

Some of our best memories center on cooking and eating. I remember awakening to the sound of my grandmother's Sunbeam stand mixer as she made the batter for waffles—a treat for us kids. What food memories do you have of your obituee?

> Sunday breakfast after church was "this big old Southern meal," son Joel said. There were the hand-rolled biscuits, cut with her husband's Thermos lid, and gravy and sausage and bacon and eggs…"Friends would ask us to stay over Saturday night and we'd say, "No. Mom's cooking." *–Louise Cook (1930–2011)*

> She especially loved the yearly Harvest Sale every October, which would sometimes fall on her birthday, the 27th. She would cook chicken and broth to make chicken & dumplings sold along with hundreds of BBQ plates. *–Ora Lee (Lemons) Hickman (1923–2017)*

[She] was famous for cooking her Filipino dish, lumpia. Every year, Charlotte would cook hundreds of lumpia for her son's marching band home competition, and even though it took her hours to get them done, they would be eaten up in just minutes. *–Charlotte Garcia Mazzo (~1962–2017)*

Home and Furnishings

Some odd items have found their way into frames in our home: my grandmother's charm bracelet, my fourth-grade composition notebook, my husband's Boy Scout canteen and pocket knife, a scrap of lace from my mother's wedding dress, and more. I've surrounded myself with memories to soothe my incurable nostalgia.

The following examples show how the obituee liked to live. Think about his or her home and zoom in. What kind of furniture do you see? Are the rooms orderly or chaotic? Which items take pride of place?

Akers presided over a dusty home filled with neatly arranged books, awards for his occasionally coherent writing and a disconnected TV. *–Autobituary, Ken Akers (?–2011)*

He was an avid reader and lifelong student of religions and philosophy. Dictionaries in English, German, [and] Latin and notebooks were always nearby. *–Gunter H. Rex (1928–2016)*

Bill loved "playing" in the garage; taking things apart, but in recent years lacked the forethought to put them back together. Including the snow blower in 500 parts that he sold for $5 at a garage sale. *–William "Bill" Frederick Radiger Sr. (1942–2016)*

Representative Objects

The objects to which a person is attached, or with which he's associated, are revealing. My grandfather always had a pipe in his pocket. My mother always has a marbled green tube of Revlon lipstick in her purse. What objects come to mind when you think of your obituee?

His signature daily regimen was to ensure he took his Gerber pocketknife, watch, wedding ring, and crucifix necklace wherever he went. *–Wayne T. Bryant (1948–2016)*

Elise was also tech-savvy, filling up her mom's i-Phone and notebook computer with a plethora of home-made videos of herself telling stories, often featuring her inseparable trio of artifacts: her pink blankie (her favorite color), her stuffed dog, "Pup-Pup," and "Cutie," her yellow rubber duckie. *–Elise Marie Korzenko (2007–2012)*

She trained parent volunteers, cajoled funding out of reluctant administrators, assembled bookcases, and even routinely carried a hammer and WD-40 in her purse for library maintenance… *–Patricia Alderson (1936–2011)*

Work

The career section of a traditional obit tends to read like a LinkedIn profile. We're regaled with a tedious list of job titles, as well as foundations and boards on which the obituee served. I found one obit that managed to use the word "committee" seven times in less than 300 words. The only thing missing was a "Connect with Steven" button.

Don't just tell us that your obituee was a blockchain systems analyst or a medical office manager or a bartender. Show us what the work was like. If he was a truck driver, for example, describe how he hauled a load of quarters under armed guard from the Denver Mint to the Tropicana Casino. Give us a day in the life:

The national news was transmitted to newspapers by the Press Wireless Company via shortwave radio and Morse code. Duffy copied the stories from the Morse transmissions and set the type for publication. *–Duffy A. Sasser (1918–2010)*

We watched her walk behind a plow leading a horse, stay on her knees for hours, thinning out carrots and weeding, milk a cow, slop the pigs, collect eggs from the chickens, [and] stand ankle deep in manure cleaning out the cow and horse stalls… *–Lucille Grossi (~1924–2010)*

She was a coroner tech, at Riverside's Sheriff coroner, her first day on the job [she] "got to hold a human heart, for a muscle its really quite squishy,"[she said]…By the 4th day she was sewing up bodies. [This is] the same person who could not be in the same room with a mouse. –*Vanessa Muñoz (1989–2016)*

He loved working in the woods and had several wood-cutting partners…He recalled the sick feeling in the pit of his stomach when they'd drop the first stick of pulpwood into the empty train boxcar, knowing they had to have it filled completely by the next day. –*Dale Marvin Nelson (1938–1909)*

Furry Friends

Pets are such an integral part of our lives that they have their own social media pages. My neighbors' new puppy, Tucker, has an Instagram account. A friend of mine set up her pugs on Twitter. And is there a wiener dog alive who doesn't have a Facebook page? Well, we'd better put them in the obituary, too:

Even Simon (the cat) knew it was time to say good-bye and was snuggled next to her on the bed when she passed. –*Virginia B. Dodd (1928–2012)*

Pat's truck, with its JILLSDAD license plates, was easily recognizable in the parking lots of local businesses as he made the rounds for mocha iced coffee, newspapers, lottery tickets and a treat for his dog, Lola, who waited patiently in the back seat. –*Pasquale J. Caramanna (1938–2016)*

She cared for all animals, especially her dog, cats and chickens that no doubt have the fanciest chicken coop in Sutter County. –*Twila LaDawn Tutrow (1962–2014)*

Passions

"We are all odd ducks in our hobbies and our obsessions, and human oddity is interesting," says William Zinsser, the author of several classic books on writing.[3] It's not the hobby itself, he says, but the "transaction" between the person and his passion that tells us something about his character:

[He] was an active participant of the American Book Collectors of Children's Books (ABCs). He delighted in dressing up for a number of years as Clifford the Big Red Dog to entertain children and their parents at the annual Connecticut Children's Book Fair at UConn. *–Richard H. Schimmelpfeng (1929–2017)*

He loved setting type on his antique presses, printing miniature books, cards, and brochures…He had a large collection of rare books on printing. He haunted antiquarian bookstores, sometimes traveling out of state to purchase a rare book to add to his collection. *–Earle H. Henness (1934–2016)*

[S]he discovered inside old crated boxes hundreds of shards of the 12' x 14' stained glass window from the chapel at Old Ursuline and worked untiringly to see this 1899 window restored to its original grandeur. *–Jean Aber (1915–2013)*

Hopes, Dreams, and Regrets

What were your obituee's loftiest ambitions? Is there something she always wanted to do or see, or a place she would have liked to visit? What would she have done differently? What long-held dreams did he or she fulfill?

She was on her way to realizing her dream of becoming a chemical engineer when she got accepted at University of the East, Manila, Philippines…However, hard times and money concerns made her decide to stop university and find work as a salesgirl in a boutique… *–Emma Burce Alfaro (1943–2014)*

Bea also did something she had always wanted to do; she tried out and got a role in the Little Theater production of *All the Way Home* at the Yakima Little Theater. She played Ma Follet. *–Beulah Hoofnagle (1932–1917)*

He had always wanted to be a stockbroker, so he took correspondence courses [and later] went to New York to finish his education…Even though his fellow classmates were the old money Ivy League types, Corky finished at the top of his class. *–Walter D. Robb (1930–1917)*

Sports

Everyone has a sports story. The first vignette below is wrought with particular skill, touching on four of the five senses:

> On Saturday morning before the game, he played the first side of the album, "Across the Field" on his record player at full volume for the entire neighborhood. At game time, he would sit on the couch in front of the TV, wrapped in a scarlet and gray, crocheted afghan blanket that was made by his sister Joan. At half-time, he would eat "gringo chili"…It was fitting that his beloved Buckeyes defeated "the team up north" [Michigan] in dramatic fashion on the last game he would watch the Saturday before he passed away. –*Robert L. Clay (1923–2016)*

> In 1937, Hackney was voted Duke's Most Valuable Player and was also honored as an All-American...[He] was touted as "The greatest running back the South has ever produced."…"This was during the time of World War II and it was amazing that such a tremendous athlete was discharged from the US Army due to a disability—"Flat Feet." –*Elmore Howard Hackney (1915–2011)*

Music

My dad played the alto sax for the National Guard band in the late '50s. He loved the soprano sax theme from *Heaven Can Wait,* his favorite movie. Shortly before he died, I downloaded the song from iTunes but (regrettably) couldn't bring myself to play it. What can I say? Music is powerful.

Was music important in your obituee's life? If so, give us the details, right down to the rosin on the bow:

> I remember my mom had an old Sears & Roebuck guitar that she used to play a few chords on and she used to sing and I would sit and watch and listen. I would try to memorize where she would hold her fingers to make the chords and then when she would lay the guitar down, I would try to remember where she put her fingers and I would spend hours and hours learning to play the guitar that way. –*Autobituary, Robert D. Blum (1934–2012)*

> He could often be found in his favorite karaoke place, 'The Junction,' laughing with his friends and telling jokes. Nathaniel

loved to sing country songs with a story or patriotic theme. Some of his favorites were: Unanswered Prayers, Chain of Love, I Thought He Walked on Water, Have You Forgotten, and Courtesy of the Red, White, and Blue. –*Nathaniel Brown Jr. (1960–2006)*

If possible, include a photo of the obituee with his or her instrument. The tribute below is accompanied by a shot of the obituee, elegantly dressed in an off-the-shoulder frock, playing her flute:

[S]he worked at the Greystone Psychiatric Hospital for 28 years as an Administrative Clinical Dietitian. Every holiday Claire performed a piano and flute Christmas concert in the Kirkbride building chapel for colleagues and their families. –*Mary Claire Braun (~1931–2015)*

Collections

Floyd "Froggy" Swank's obituary captures our interest instantly. Mr. Swank—shall we call him "Froggy"?—was a lifelong resident of Painesville, Ohio. By rights, though, he should have been born and bred in Dixie. Froggy was a "God-fearing Christian," worked as a cook at a Perkins restaurant, and collected "frogs, unusual tea pots, [and] Jeff Gordon knick-knacks." (If you collect NASCAR memorabilia, ya might be a redneck…)

Fact is, most of us collect something. What we keep and how we display it can be revealing. Give an example or two of the items your obituee collected, and be specific: include its model name, color, date, shape, labeling, or other relevant details:

[He] collected [National Geographic] magazines and read them daily. One of his favorite issues contained a picture of a black rhino. A highlight for Gregory was a recent outing to the zoo to see a black rhino in person. –*Gregory Kosse (~1923–2014)*

His favorite thing was collecting his "toys." He collected everything from McDonalds toys to Legos, Hot Wheels to vintage autos and Harley Davidsons. He loved having something someone else wanted. –*Ramsey Paul Wamble (1967–2016)*

She maintained a collection of empty See's Candies boxes and Miracle Whip jars because they "might come in handy for something." *–Jean Masamori (?–2015)*

He had a passion for collecting antique milk bottles and was very proud of his milk bottle collection, numbering about 3,500 bottles from the state of Ohio. Lou's bottles, procured over the past 30 years, were widely recognized in the state and beyond as a unique and unusual collection. *–Louis B. McFadden (1937–2013)*

I can't help thinking that Ms. Masamori and Mr. McFadden would have gotten on splendidly with Froggy.

CAN WE TALK?

To gather information, you need to get others talking. Try an app like StoryCorps, which "enables anyone, anywhere to record meaningful conversations with another person." Or use the following list of questions. It's intended to draw out the kinds of details we've just talked about. These questions can work whether you're interviewing the obituee, speaking to one of his or her family members, or answering the questions for your own obituary. Every situation is different—adapt the questions to fit your circumstances:

- What was the obituee's nickname, and how did he or she get it?

- In what ways did his personality and values change over the years?

- Whom did the obituee admire or despise, and why?

- What events shaped your obituee's outlook on life?

- How would you describe the obituee's role in the family? Supply a brief story to illustrate.

- Describe a family legend or running joke.

- How did your obituee meet his or her spouse?

- What were the obituee's favorite phrases?

- What philosophy or motto did the obituee live by?

- What kind of volunteer work did the obituee do?

- In what ways did her appearance change over the years?

- What color was the obituee's hair when he or she was young? Describe its style—bouffant, crew cut, shag, etc.

- Did he ever have a beard of moustache?

- What did the person typically wear (be specific about colors, fabrics, or other material), and what did those choices say about him or her?

- Describe how the obituee moved. How did she enter a room? What gestures were typical of her?

- What was he like when annoyed, worried, or angry?

- What do you remember about the way your obituee spoke?

- What scents or smells do you associate with your obituee? Pipe smoke? Axle grease? AquaVelva? Hot boiled peanuts?

- What textures do you associate with the obituee and the things around him?

- What did your obituee like to eat and cook? Is there a family recipe that you associate with her?

- Was your obituee tidy or disorganized?

- Was your obituee a cat person or a dog person?

- What object best encapsulates who the obituee was? It might be a watch or a piece of jewelry, an article of clothing, an item in her home, or something she always had with her.

- What items were you likely to find in her handbag (or in his briefcase or pocket), and what do they say about her?

- What did your obituee's work mean to him or her?

- What was his favorite way to spend free time?

- What special talent or skill was he most proud of?

- What did your obituee wish she had devoted less time to?

- Was there something or somewhere your obituee dreamed of that she never had the chance to do, see, or become?

- What hobbies did your obituee have, or what sports did he participate in? (Be specific!)

- What kind of music did your obituee like, and why? Did he play an instrument?

- What did the obituee collect? How was the collection displayed?

Chapter 5

THE BARF DRAFT
C'mon, Let It All Out

There will always be some happy-go-lucky folks who take life as it comes and are content to leave behind no more than a shellacked fish mounted on plywood. But I'm betting most of you are more like me—neurotic types who lie awake at night wondering whether we've accomplished anything worth remembering.

Insomnia doesn't slow the hourglass, though, and the day of reckoning eventually arrives. As the obituarist, it's your task to spotlight the obituee's contributions and capture his or her essence—quirks and all (see Chapter 4). But how to begin?

WHY THE BARF DRAFT IS YOUR FRIEND

A good story, says radio producer Bradley Campbell, is told the way you'd speak to a friend. So why not start with your phone? He suggests you run through your story from start to finish with the recorder rolling, and then transcribe the recording (or use an app to transcribe it for you). The result is a working document he calls a "barf draft."[1] "You look at it and you're like 'Oh, this isn't scary,'" he says. "It's just…a really, really terrible first draft."

You can use Campbell's technique to concoct a barf draft of your obituary. The result might be a garbled string of all the stories and factoids you've scrounged together. That's okay. The point is to produce some raw material you can massage into shape. "I can fix a bad page," says author Nora Roberts. "I can't fix a blank page."

Some people seize up when they're being recorded. I'm one of them. If you're the same way, put your barf draft in writing instead. Think of it as a mental throwdown in which you cast aside all concern for spelling, grammar, punctuation, and word choice. Leave a placeholder if you're missing a fact or detail, as I've done in the draft below. Don't fuss over the sequence of your ideas, either. "Get your facts first," said Mark Twain. "Then you can distort them as you please."

The passage below is the barf draft of my mother's pre-need obituary. It proves that Hemingway was spot-on when he told a younger writer that "the first draft of anything is shit."[2] With my mindmap handy, I turned each item (the underlined words and phrases) into a sentence or brief story. Voilà! A 500-word barf draft:

> Judy would put on <u>lipstick</u> just to go out and get the mail. You always knew when she was finished getting ready in the morning, because the scent of <u>Shalimar</u> would drift out of the bathroom. She was proud of her trim figure and had tremendous "will power," as she put it, to resist temptation. She'd cut a <u>Hostess cupcake</u> into quarters and make it her dessert for a week. She kept her hair and makeup just so, giving herself <u>Toni home perms</u> every few weeks.
>
> Judy had an utter lack of squeamishness. When the kids were older, she became the lab manager at Belleville Area College. The lab kept live frogs and rats on hand for dissection. One Sunday afternoon, when Judy went in to feed them, she turned on the

lights and discovered that the <u>frogs</u> had escaped and promptly dried out, their bodies strewn about the lab. Unphased, Judy peeled the frogs off of desks, countertops, and concrete floors and cleaned up the mess.

Judy kept herself in wonderful physical condition by volunteering as a <u>gardener</u> at her X-acre condominium complex. She and her husband Richard never fulfilled their dream of sailing around the world, but they came close. They enjoyed more than a decade (?) of cruising on their <u>boat</u>, Ti Lok (a Thai word meaning "mistress"). While on shore or on one of their many <u>road trips</u>, they hit museum after museum—<u>art museums</u> were their favorite, but they went to X, X, and X.

Judy sparkled. Throughout her life, she sparkled in the company of others—literally, in her signature <u>sequined</u> tops and bracelets, and figuratively, while enjoying a good conversation and a glass of bubbly. She was a wonderful <u>hostess</u> and genuinely enjoyed "having company" for dinner or cocktails.

Judy won the XX Science Fair with an <u>experiment</u> showing that lab rats fed X grew larger and stronger than a control group of rats given X. She killed the rats with poison and measured them. This effort earned her a full scholarship to Illinois College, where she majored in biology.

Over a period of 50 years, she and Richard <u>moved 22 times</u> and lived in eight states, relocating with no more fuss than folks packing a few ham sandwiches for a day at the lake. With the lab experience now on her résumé, she worked as a pharmaceutical <u>salesperson</u> and later as a medical equipment salesperson, winning the presidents club award many times.

In her seventies, Judy's top priority was her only <u>grandchild</u>, Richard. She homeschooled him throughout most of high school. He was the bright planet around whom her life revolved. When she wasn't with him, she was out with friends or on the <u>phone</u>.

For Judy, <u>cleaning</u> and organizing were hobbies. She was so efficient that you could take a bowl out of the cabinet, and she'd whisk away your "dirty" dish in the time it took you to retrieve a box of cereal.

Now, this draft is dreadful: The paragraphs are sloppy, the word choices clumsy, and the structure as clear as hot dog water. But now, at least, I have something to work with.

REVAMPING YOUR BARF DRAFT

A modern obit invites you in, shows you what was special about the obituee, and brings the tribute to a neat close—in other words, its principal parts are the intro, body, and conclusion. In a virtual memorial or life review, you might go down a dozen other rabbit holes to create supplementary content—a timeline or "chapters," a bereavement diary, messages for loved ones, and so on. The following sections refer only to the text-centered portion of your tribute. See Chapters 9 and 10 to learn about features and media for your digital memorial or life review.

In my experience, it's easier to introduce and wrap up a piece after you know what it says, so I like to begin with the body. If you already have a fantastic hook in mind, though, start there. Or hammer out a conclusion and work backward. "There are all kinds of writers and all kinds of methods," says William Zinsser in *On Writing Well,* "and any method that works is the right one for you."[3]

The Hook

An obit needs curb appeal. Even in newspapers, the opening line or two of an obituary is prime real estate. This narrow strip is even more valuable in an online obit. The reason is simple: On a mobile device, only the beginning of the piece appears on screen. Your hook must prompt readers to click through to the remaining content. And you'd better pull them in quickly: According to Amazon's Alexa, a competitive intelligence tool (not the Alexa who orders your toothpaste), the average Legacy.com visitor spends just under 3 minutes on the site.[4]

Give your readers a tour of the rooms that made your obituee a one-of-a-kind structure. Let folks peek inside the closets and check out the fridge. Writing a snappy intro is crazy hard—I get it. But to produce a superb send-off, you have to sell it.

Robert McG. Thomas Jr., legendary *New York Times* obituarist of the downtrodden, understood the value of an enticing hook. The opening sentence of each "McG," as his pieces were known, gave a thumbnail of the obituee's entire life:

Sylvia Weinberger, who used a sprinkling of matzoh meal, a pinch of salt and a dollop of schmaltzmanship to turn chopped liver into a commercial success, died on July 23 at a hospital in Fort Lauderdale, Fla.

Betty James, who came up with the name Slinky for the stair-walking spring that has delighted children for more than 60 years and who ran the toy company after her husband, the inventor, left it and his family in 1960, died Thursday in Philadelphia.

Mason Rankin, a Salt Lake City businessman who had such an abundance of compassion for people with AIDS that he kept scores of volunteer knitters furiously clicking away to supply afghans, sweaters, scarves, and hats to people in Utah's H.I.V. community, died on Sept. 21 at a hospital in Salt Lake City.

The "who" clause became Thomas's schtick—it must have tickled him to shoehorn so much info into a single sentence. The result can be a little impersonal, but Thomas does show us how to cannonball right into the story. He might have admired these intriguing hooks:

One of the few advantages of dying from Grade 3, Stage IIIC endometrial cancer, recurrent and metastasized to the liver and abdomen, is that you have time to write your own obituary. (The other advantages are no longer bothering with sunscreen and no longer worrying about your cholesterol.) *–Jane Catherine Lotter (1953–2013)*

Glenn Grise was heard yelling, "Wahoo! What a ride… Somebody woo me," as he crossed to the other side on Jan. 31, 2017. What a ride it has been. *–Glenn Grise (1962–2017)*

Ann would like to let you know that her work here is done. She received a call, a sort of an offer you can't refuse, for an appointment from which she will not be returning. This assignment comes with a huge sign-on bonus, a reunion with family and friends she has not seen in a long time. Job security is exactly 110 percent. *–Nevena Ann Topic (?–2013)*

In lieu of a hook, virtual memorials (see Chapter 8) offer templates similar to this one:

> This tribute is dedicated in loving memory of [name], [age], born on [date], who passed away on [date]. We will remember [him/her] forever....

How very touching.

The bracketed fields populate with the information you supply when you set up the account. Nearly every intro on the site is identical, save for the obituee's name, age, and date of death. Trying to find a single inspiring sentence among all those joyless leads is a painful, fruitless task.

For crying out loud! Did Al Gore invent the internet so we could churn out these gloomy mad-libs? Thankfully, the templates are editable, the tepid language only a (bad) suggestion. Vaporize it. Then start over with a real lead.

Scan your barf draft and your unused material—interviews, notes, social media posts, and so on—for a zingy quotation, vivid image, or colorful snippet you can use as a hook. Here are some ideas from real obituaries. (Not all of the examples appeared as the hook in their respective tributes, but perhaps they should have.)

- Describe a favorite photograph. Mr. Redpath's obit is accompanied by a snapshot of the beaming 82-year-old giving the "Hang Ten" sign:

> "Aloha," a smile, a hard pat on the back, and a handshake were how Peter B. Redpath greeted family friends, and strangers. *–Peter B. Redpath (~1934–2016)*

- Disclose something surprising:

> Once, getting caught unawares...on a nude beach in France, she wisely observed [that] "it's always better to leave something to the imagination." *–Kathryn Davis Grado (~1936–2016)*

- Start with something funny:

  William Ziegler escaped this mortal realm on Friday, July 29, 2016 at the age of 69. We think he did it on purpose to avoid having to make a decision in the pending presidential election. *–William Ziegler (~1947–2016)*

- Begin with an anecdote—a brief tale that illustrates the obituee's character or personality. Describe an unlikely achievement, mortifying predicament, wrong turn, joyful or heartbreaking event, unthinkable hardship, humorous misunderstanding, or youthful debacle:

  When Nick was diagnosed [with Lou Gehrig's disease], he was on a cross country road trip with a group of friends traveling down the west coast. From that point forward, he chose to use his body as a canvas, as he realized he would soon have difficulty communicating. Two of his first post-diagnosis tattoos were done in script on the back of his hands—"Don't Worry" on the left, and "Be Happy" on the right. This was his life's motto. *–Nicholas Michael Bellotti (1984–2016)*

  David Margolis had only been a federal prosecutor for four years when he found himself negotiating the surrender of a gun-toting bank robber on a Connecticut baseball field. The fugitive, Walter "Tippy" Doolittle, said he was willing to give himself up; the proviso was that he would only surrender to [the young prosecutor, who looked like a fellow hippie]. *–David Margolis (~1940–2016)*

- Give the obituee's motto or describe the lessons she taught:

  If you're about to throw away an old pair of pantyhose, stop… We were blessed to learn many valuable lessons from Pink during her 85 years, among them: Never throw away old pantyhose. Use the old ones to tie gutters, child-proof cabinets, tie toilet flappers, or hang Christmas ornaments. *–Mary A. "Pink" Mullaney (~1928–1913)*

Held the world in a paper cup—drank it up. *–Nancy Elaine Stolba Winitzky (1948–2008)*

A popular saying at our house was, "waste not, want not, eat it up, wear it out, make it do, or do without." Mission accomplished, Dad. *–Robert W. Brooks (1930–2012)*

- Recall a typical gesture or movement:

When his dad sung him "Row, Row, Row Your Boat" [Oliver] would emphatically row his little boat and clap his hands with joy. *–Oliver Johannes Garza (2014–2015)*

The Body

Paragraphs

To organize your draft, you'll need to be on friendly terms with the paragraph. Bear with me for a quick-and-dirty refresher, or skip ahead if you don't need it.

Paragraphs are nifty organizational units for presenting cohesive ideas and thoughts. Each paragraph consists of a topic sentence followed by supporting details. The topic sentence is like a trenchcoat covering the package of specifics beneath it.

When you're writing for an online audience, it's best to keep your paragraphs short. Our online and mobile reading habits are different from our print reading habits. One study found that the average web page visitor reads only 20%–28% of the words on the screen.[5]

Shorter sentences and paragraphs are easier for the mobile reader to absorb as he or she eyeballs the page. The U.S. government usability office recommends that each paragraph be no longer than five sentences, and that each sentence contain no more than 20 words.[6] Digital content specialist Tyrus Manuel recommends "strategically breaking up paragraphs."[7]

The ideal paragraph moves from broad (the overcoat) to particular (the boxers or briefs beneath it). Of course, not every paragraph is so tidy, but that's the pattern you're after:

Arch was passionate about food…He made several wedding cakes and many birthday cakes (or sometimes chocolate mousse, snickerdoodles, or fruit tarts at the request of the birthday child). Most of all he loved to visit local markets and to try new foods—from Australian Witchetty grubs and fried ants to elegant five-course meals at 3-star Michelin restaurants. *—Archibald John Allen III (1942–2017)*

Heather had a passion for debate and discussion. Whether you wanted to defend foreign policy decisions or debate the value of the designated hitter, if you wanted to have a discussion with Heather, you had to be prepared to defend your position…On the eve of an election she had some friends who would simply call [her] and ask, "How should I vote tomorrow?" They never had to worry that she wouldn't have an opinion. *—Heather Alvarez (1977–2014)*

White Space

The indentation or skipped line at the end of each paragraph is a visual cue that you're shifting to a new thought or idea. If you have any control over the design of your obituary or digital memorial page, skip a line between paragraphs and use wide margins. White space—unused space on the screen—is visually important in attracting and retaining readers. "White space rests the eye, separates chunks of information, and makes a document look inviting," say Darlene Smith-Worthington and Sue Jefferson, authors of *Technical Writing for Success.*[8]

Themes

Eyeball your draft for themes or motifs in your obituee's life. For example, the ideas in my mom's pre-need obit fit neatly into three broad categories, each illustrating an aspect of her personality: vivaciousness, levelheadedness, and curiosity (about science in her professional life and the arts in her personal life).

In choosing your themes, avoid falling back on the everyman stereotypes you find in traditional obituaries—loving father, loyal company man. We don't want to read about Walter Mitty. We want to know about his secret life. Look for unpredictable roles: fixer, spendthrift, diva, defector, underdog. Be creative.

Sequence and Transitions

Once you've organized your material into related ideas, it's time to sequence them and find ways to transition smoothly from one paragraph to the next. Remember, every life has an obvious narrative arc: It begins at birth and ends at death. (For those of you who weren't English majors, the narrative arc is just the storyline, as in "rags to riches" or "boy meets girl.") But that doesn't mean you have to write the obituary in that order.

In fact, researchers have found that we pay more attention and have better recall when a story doesn't move in a straight line.[9] That's why movie directors use nonlinear techniques like flashbacks, dream sequences, and shifting perspectives. They know that a little choppiness amps up tension and suspense. Just be sure you pivot logically to bring the reader along with you:

- Compare or contrast ("Likewise," "On the other hand," "Nevertheless")
- Show cause and effect ("The result was predictable," "Because she grew up without a mother…")
- Transition to a new time, place, or situation ("In the meantime," "The first time she ever tried X," "Next thing you knew," "When it was over," "In the end")

The Conclusion

Your conclusion should echo one of your themes or circle back to your hook, bringing the story to a satisfying close. "Like a poem's final stanza," says writer Francis Flaherty, "the end of a story can linger in memory,"[10] as in this wrenching example:

> Nate used to debate his boys about who loved whom the most. Daniel, a big fan of Buzz Lightyear, told his dad, "I love you to infinity and beyond." Nate, momentarily stumped, came back with, "I love you to infinity and beyond... and back again!" That phrase became a part of Nate's permanent bond with his children. Nate, that's how much we all loved you. And miss you. *–Nathan Paul Bahner (1978–2012)*

If that passage didn't get you a little *verklemmt*, you are a monster, my friend.

Despite its sentimentality, this conclusion works because it's not just a heap of adjectives. The obituarist doesn't simply tell us that Mr. Bahner was a "loving father" who "took great joy in his family" and "never complained." (If I had a dime for every time I've read one of those phrases...) Instead, with a tender anecdote and poignant quotations, it shows us Mr. Bahner's interaction with his children, riffing on themes introduced in the body of the tribute.

A traditional obituary concludes with an announcement of the funeral arrangements and a list of surviving family members. I recommend that you not include those sections at all. A request for memorial donations is optional. Let's take a closer look.

Survivors

In my dad's obituary, I included a cumbersome list of surviving family members and their spouses. Such lists are stubborn remnants of a time when communities relied on newspapers to announce and record important events. The internet has made it pointless to offer such information. In the unlikely event someone would actually need a list of survivors, that information is available elsewhere online.

If you want to name the obituee's close family members on the grounds that they were part of his or her life, try to work the names into the text, like so, instead listing them outright:

> Her early years were spent on a farm where she was known to adopt and nurture sick animals. Hazel's brother, Robert Wesley Rice, was 13 years her senior, and rode a horse to school. She always wanted to have a horse, but the closest she came was coaxing a blind old mare to the fence, where she could climb on her back. *–Hazel Maurine Roggy (1923–2016)*

Funeral Arrangements

Unlike a traditional newspaper obit, an online obit or virtual memorial remains available as a permanent tribute to the deceased. Any text devoted to funeral arrangements, then, becomes obsolete once the service has taken place. Your word count may have no limits, but your reader's attention does.

Besides, the mortuary that handles the funeral or memorial service will post the time and date of the services on its website and submit an announcement to the local newspaper. Repeating the info in your obit is unnecessary.

Some virtual memorial templates include sidebars for funeral arrangements. This separation keeps the text of your tribute readable and highlights the arrangements. The sidebar can be hidden from view after the service takes place.

A notification app such as Everdays is a handy way to spread the news about funeral or memorial arrangements. The app sends a contemporary-looking announcement by text or email to the contacts you select. Your contacts need not have the app installed to receive the notification, but those who do will receive an in-app notification instead. These apps have RSVP features and can update mourners if the date, time, or location of the service changes.

Some apps will let you follow a particular funeral home, so that you'll be notified if anyone in your community or circle dies. This feature is useful for folks who live in small towns that have only one or two mortuaries. See Chapter 8 for more on apps and virtual memorials.

In Lieu of Flowers

The phrase "in lieu of flowers" first appeared as an effort by some families to divert funds that would otherwise be "wasted" on flowers. It became so commonplace that most obituarists now include it unthinkingly. In the past decade or so, the phrase has become a meme, of sorts:

> In lieu of flowers, go to a [Chicago] CUBS game and raise your glass in memory of Mary. –*Mary Fickenscher (1928–2016)*

> In lieu of flowers, please make memorial contributions to "Tom Brady's Deflategate Defense." –*Barbara "GiGi" Shippee (~1941–2015)*

> In lieu of flowers, John requested that you please vote for ANYONE but Donald Trump, because he will roll over in his

grave if Mr. Trump is elected! (This message was authorized and approved by John prior to his death!) *–John Dales (1961–2016)*

The Society of American Florists points out that most people continue to send flowers in sympathy despite the prevalence of the "irksome phrase" discouraging it.[11] When my dad died, one of my best customers sent me a flower arrangement. I was really touched at this kind show of sympathy. I hadn't expected anything more than perhaps a nice email.

Some economists say the expenditure on sympathy flowers is a massive misallocation of resources. It's certainly a ginormous market. In 2015, the floral industry was an $18 billion segment of the U.S. economy.[12] Sympathy flowers represent about 20% of the total in any given year.[13] On average, American households spend about $49 annually on fresh flowers.[14] (In 2017, for example, U.S. consumers spent $2 billion on Valentine's Day flowers.[15] Hey, guys, here's a tip: We'd rather have donuts. But I digress.)

Environmentalists don't like the floral industry, either. They grumble about the huge carbon footprint left by transporting carnations from Cartagena, Colombia, where almost 80% of imported flowers are grown, to far-flung places like Bangor and Baton Rouge. Citing these objections, some large employers refuse to reimburse expenses for sympathy flowers—not even for an employee's funeral.[16]

Following are some creative requests you might make of mourners:

- Bring a book to donate to a local nursing home or children's hospital.
- Fund the purchase of library books (digital or print) on the obituee's favorite topic.
- Plant a tree in honor of the deceased.
- Donate a toy for a mini–toy drive in the obituee's name.
- Visit a nursing home resident or elderly neighbor who has no family.
- Launch a Kickstarter campaign to defray funeral expenses or to set up an educational trust for the

obituee's children or grandchildren (see Chapter 8 for more on crowdfunding).

- Join an organ donor registry. (For instructions, contact the organ donation advocacy group in your state, province, or county.)

These suggestions needn't be made in lieu of flowers, though. "Why not beef up the bank accounts of the folks at the Society of American Florists[17]," says Barbara Field, a writer at the University of California–San Diego. "They're not a bad bunch."

Chapter 6

THE DAZZLE IS IN THE DETAILS
Writing in Hi-Res

"You must write as if Dostoevsky himself will be reading your [writing], and Shakespeare will be acting it out," says Christina Westover in her novel *Precipice*. But hey, no pressure.

If you've moved through this book in order, you now have a serviceable obituary in hand. You brainstormed, collected anecdotes and factoids, wrote a crummy draft, and reorganized it into related themes and cohesive paragraphs. You gave it a brilliant hook, and you closed the piece with panache. Now you're ready for some spit 'n' polish. Let's make it shine.

"I think the best obits now and forever will be the ones that touch the reader through revealing, riveting details," says obituaries editor Adam Bernstein.[1] A vibrant word buoys an obituary. Vague, sullen verbiage drags it down like concrete shoes. Specificity is the hallmark of good writing:

General: The boys loved baseball.

Specific: They rode the streetcar to Lane Field on Sundays to watch Padre double headers… *–Charles Nathaniel Ables (1921–2012)*

General: She was a wonderful seamstress.

Specific: Janina created debutante, quinceañera, and tailored dresses for women and girls. *–Janina Berrocal-Lopez (1929–2012)*

General: He sold a variety of hardware items to stores throughout the region.

Specific: Driving his red van, with the CB radio handle of "Clothespin," he [sold clothesline at] hardware stores and boatyards across the state…He also had ventures in masking tape, meat hooks (for the backyard grille) and oars that were seconds, warped and of odd lengths that were best used for firewood. He is survived by his signature license plate, "ROPE." *–John Austin Amory (1924–2013)*

ADDING SPECIFICITY

How do you move from generic to precise? Let's unpack the process one word at a time. Then you can apply the same steps as you spiff up your draft.

First, consider the verb—the action word—in each sentence. Look at the difference a more precise verb makes:

> Every day Heather *rode* her bike down the road.
> Every day Heather *raced* down the road on her bike.

Don't hesitate to rearrange the other words in the sentence as necessary, as I've done above.

Now think about each noun (person, place, or thing) in your sentence. Heather is the subject—no need for more specificity there. But let's improve "day," "bike" and "road." You can replace the noun with a more specific one, like this:

> Every *morning* Heather raced down the road on her bike.

74

Or you can add a descriptor to make the noun more specific:

> Every morning Heather raced down the *rutted gravel road* on her bike.

Or do both. Here I've changed the noun from "bike" to "Schwinn Stingray," and I've added "mighty" to describe it.

> Every morning Heather raced down the rutted gravel road on her *mighty Schwinn Stingray.*

Better, eh? We're almost there. Now let's add some sensory imagery. When you picture Heather, what else do you see in your mind's eye? Since we're making this up, there are no wrong answers. You can use characteristics like color, size, temperature, speed, movement, sound, flavor, or light to describe the scene:

> Every morning Heather raced down the rutted gravel road on her mighty Schwinn Stingray, *streamers flying and tires crunching, a plume of white dust at her back.*

Try not to reach for the first sensory impressions that come to mind. If you do that, you'll end up writing that the sun was shining and the sky was blue, or some such drivel.

If you do use an obvious image—the wind was blowing, the birds were singing, that sort of thing—at least make your description unique. You could say something like "a slipstream of cool air washed over her" or "the trill of a wood thrush announced her takeoff." If you can't verify a trivial detail—was it a wood thrush or a pine warbler?—take your best guess. Call it poetic license.

If you're rusty on your parts of speech, don't worry—you don't need to know a noun from a knapsack. For any given word, just drill down. For instance, if you've written that your parents met when your mom spilled a drink on your dad's pants, consider what kind of drink it was and what kind of pants he was wearing. You might end up with "spilled a highball on his gray flannel trousers" or "spilled a mint julep on his Bermuda shorts," or whatever the case may be. Easy peasy.

Using Brand Names

We live in a consumer society, and brand names have strong nostalgic associations. Consider the popularity of vintage goods on Etsy and eBay. We watch Antiques Roadshow, American Pickers, and Pawn Stars not just for the fun of the treasure hunt, but also for the nostalgic tug of seeing the G.I. Joes, Tinkertoys, and Easy-Bake Ovens we played with as kids.

When I think of my grandparents, I can still smell the Zest soap in the hall bath. I can see, hear, and smell—but as a child, wasn't allowed to taste—the Dana Brown Safari Coffee percolating in the Mr. Coffee machine. (With my current 8-cup daily ration of home-brewed Starbucks, I'm making up for lost time).

The takeaway is simple: whether it's a toy, a watch, or a shoe, give the brand name:

> Chieffi is looking down on us and smiling. His hair is red again, he's wearing a new pair of Converse Chuck Taylors, has a Bacardi and Pepsi with fresh ice in one hand, and is saying, "How you like me now?" *–James M. Chieffi (1948–2012)*

> As he flew around the country, he carried a large Samsonite suitcase with a drafting board, sliding ruler, drafting tools, architectural spec book for figuring loads, and a light bulb to replace the dim motel bulb at night. *–Richard Claywell (1936–2016)*

> She wore out two KitchenAid MixMasters… *–Lois Nichols Henley (1914–2010)*

Adding Quotations

A quotation might describe the way someone looked, walked, talked, or put out a cigarette. The idea, says obituary writer Sandra Martin, is to make your obituee "breathe once more on the page"[2]—or screen, as it were:

Dad didn't believe in allowances. He'd always say; "If you want to earn some money, just ask me." When we did, he'd grab his clip board and take us on a tour. "See that flower bed?" he'd ask, "That's worth $10." *–Robert William Casparie (1916–2011)*

In my teen years I would stop by my dad's store and we would go upstairs and watch for shoplifters. When we would see someone put something in their pockets, Dad would get on the intercom and say, "Young man on Aisle 3, put back that item." The young man would look all over to see who was watching [him]. Dad would get back on the intercom and say, "Yes, you." *–John "Jack" Thomas Sullivan (1933–2012)*

Dad used to quote Sergeant Schultz from the TV show Hogan's Heroes saying, "I know nothing," but that was far from the truth, as he was an avid reader and took continual enrichment courses. "You can never have enough schooling," he would say. *–Luis Reuben Apodaca (1946–2015)*

If you quote from a movie, book, song, or other creative work, remember to give credit to the original author:

"It is said that your life flashes before your eyes just before you die," writes Terry Pratchett in *The Last Continent*. "That is true, it's called Life."

Including the title of the book or speech that contains the quotation is good practice but not mandatory, especially if the line has been widely quoted:

"I am ready to meet my maker," said Winston Churchill. "Whether my maker is prepared for the great ordeal of meeting me is another matter."

Making Comparisons

"Dying is a wild night and a new road," said Oscar Wilde. Groovy metaphor. But most comparisons used in obituaries are sappy enough to glaze a cinnamon bun. She lit up the room, sang like an angel, and had eyes as blue as the ocean. *Ugh.*

Done right, a comparison can add another layer of subtlety to your portrait. Use fresh, original images that tie in to your theme. If your obituee was a veteran, try military metaphors. If she was a teacher, go down that corridor. Your obituee loved to travel? Allude to journeys, exploration, and discovery.

Here are some original comparisons with strong thematic tie-ins:

He felt a cluttered environment caused a cluttered mind, which led to wasted time. His home, car and garage were like a library's Dewey decimal system. *–Michael A Bailey (?–2015)*

"He went out like a Marine," she told a friend on the phone hours after her son's death. "Swift and silent." *–Ethan Alexander Arbelo (2001–2014)*

The battle [with Parkinson's disease] for her was not so much a "fight," but more like a never-ending dance, approached with child-like grace. *–Nancy Arbosheski (~1935–2014)*

She traveled to 19 countries, wandered ancient ruins, and encountered wildlife from sloths and anteaters to pink dolphins. She was fearless and even went on a successful search for anaconda. Like a tropical flower herself, Christy stood out for her colorful headscarves, even before she was diagnosed with inflammatory breast cancer in 2012. *–Christy Lyn Bailey (1967–2015)*

Stan Avery said of their partnership, "Our natures were balanced like a well-tuned gyroscope. I supplied the imagination and Russ the reality that kept us in business." *–H. Russell Smith (1914–2014)*

USING HUMOR

Some readers are alarmed or offended at the idea that an obituary can (and perhaps should) be funny. That's understandable. After a devastating loss, it's hard to eat, sleep, and breathe, much less laugh. But as George Bernard Shaw once observed, life doesn't stop being funny when someone dies or stop being serious when someone laughs.

When Meg McSherry began writing obituaries for the *Chicago Tribune,* she remarked that "even the most sorrowful relatives, if given a chance, will break into laughter or animated storytelling when they recall [their loved ones'] lives."[3]

Even a failed attempt at lightheartedness beats a successful attempt at blandness. But some of the best lines are those written in earnest by obituarists who aren't trying to be funny:

> Of all his work, his service and awards he received, Larry would tell you his proudest accomplishment was the cooperative work he did to eradicate the screw worm. *–Larry Leonard Fernandes (1924–2017)*

(To be fair, that blasted screw worm can do a helluva lot of damage.)

Reach for a little sly, tongue-in-cheek humor when you see an opening. One man wrote his father's entire obit in that vein:

> Wayne Neal has exited his rickety old body, having lived twice as long as he expected and way longer than he deserved. *–Howard Wayne Neal (~1942–2016)*

Writers with a flair for humor often deliver it drily:

> His curiosity [as a child] landed him in boarding school after an experiment gone wrong blew up his father's victory garden and his mother caught him trying to save the cat population by learning how to perform feline appendectomies. *–William Bryant Bailey (1928–2015)*

> Charlie's version of hunting consisted of dressing in his bright orange clothing, walking into the woods and sitting at the base of a tree to have a good nap. It's anyone's guess how many deer took a look at him, sneered in the way only a deer might, and then trotted on, knowing they were safe when they came across Charlie. *–Charles Irwin Pressey (1944–2016)*

> He despised phonies, his 1969 Volvo (which he also loved), know-it-all Yankees, Southerners who used the words "veranda" and

"porte cochere" to put on airs, eating grape leaves, Law and Order (all franchises), cats, and Martha Stewart. In reverse order. *–Harry Stamps (1932–2013)*

A study in the *Journal of Memory and Language* claims that humor is baked in to certain words, even apart from their meaning.[4] The researchers theorize that a word like "canoodling" would be funny even if it had nothing to do with fooling around. If true, these findings would explain why children dig Dr. Seuss.[5]

All other things being equal, opt for words and phrases that pack a comedic punch. Certain words beginning with "k" or a "k" sound—kiester, kravat, kvetch—are reliably funny. But I can't overstate the importance of reading your writing out loud. Once you do it a few times, you'll agree that words spoken out loud sound different from those you hear in your mind's ear.

WHAT NOT TO WRITE

Dangerously Cheesy

Sentimental words and phrases are like Oreos—handy, satisfying morsels we can consume in great quantity without much thought. An original turn of phrase is more like an underripe banana. It's not quite there at first. But come back to it in a day or two, and you might have something sweet.

When Stephen Lock was obituaries editor of the *British Medical Journal*, he published a set of guidelines for those tasked with writing a colleague's obituary. In it he included an amusing list of phrases he was weary of seeing, such as "Adored/beloved by all his/her staff/patients/colleagues." "Nobody wants old scores paid off in spiteful, dismissive passages," he said, "but, equally, a recital of glib stock phrases is just as inadequate."[6]

In that spirit, I'd like to offer my own list of tiresome phrases. If you still want to use them, fine. This isn't a blacklist. Just be aware of the high schlock factor associated with them:

- Was larger than life
- Never knew a stranger

- Captured everyone's heart
- Will be greatly/sadly missed
- Touched everyone he/she met
- Had a smile that lit up the room
- Would have done anything for anybody
- Would have given you the shirt off his back
- Was adored by everyone who knew him/her
- Was a devoted/loyal friend [or father, aunt, etc.]
- Had a [smile/laugh] that was [contagious/ infectious]

Eternally Hokey

Euphemisms are clichés that spare us from more direct language. Mabel "left this earth for greener pastures," "went home to be with the Lord," "departed this life," "entered eternal rest," etc. Out with it! Mabel is deader than DVDs.

If you're going to use a euphemism, at least be creative: the deceased has "hung up his tool belt," "laid down her cutting shears," or "fried her last latke." Here are some other playful examples:

> The Reverend Gary Thompson Schubert—doughnut locavore, explorer, car enthusiast, man of the people, and man of God—received an offer he could not refuse on Saturday, June 27, 2015.

> Elwood "Buddy" Segeske III, age 60, former soccer player, tool and die maker, and David Bowie look-alike, ate his last soft pretzel on February 25th, 2016.

> John Selfridge, a mathematician's mathematician and a bon vivant's bad-boy, has found his last prime number and sung his last Al Jolsen song.

LIFTING THE ADVERB EMBARGO

"The road to hell is paved with adverbs," says Stephen King.[7] You may have heard the argument for taking this "runt of the grammatical litter" out to slaughter. An adverb—loosely defined, is a word that describes how, how much, how many, or when. It's a throwaway, according to its detractors. A lazy filler for insecure writers. An unnecessary hedge. Writers in this camp say that instead of using an adverb, you choose simply choose a stronger verb.

Take our earlier example, "Heather rode her bike." We could have added an adverb to make "rode" more specific: "Heather rode quickly," for example. "Quickly" is an adverb telling us *how* Heather rode. Instead, we chose a stronger verb: "Heather raced." But as Lily Rothman points out in *The Atlantic,* sometimes your verb can't be any more precise: "A sigh is just a sigh," she says, "but anyone who has ever been in love knows how important it is to distinguish between when she sighs happily and when she sighs otherwise."[8]

Good writing is conversational, and our conversations are punctuated with adverbs. Try to have even a simple exchange—describing your vacation plans, say—without using "just," "really," "a little," "pretty" (as in "pretty sweet"), "probably," "usually," or "already." Go ahead, try it.

Impossible, right? The claim that adverbs weaken your writing is "misguided," says Maddie Crum, of the *Huffington Post.* "Adverbs," she says, "can be phonetically pleasing, can imbue sentences with subtlety, and should not be entirely shunned."[9] *Bah-DUM-bum.* (If you caught Ms. Crum's little play on words there, consider yourself a grammar nerd.) There's a reason the adverb is one of the eight parts of speech: We speak with it. Why should we not write with it?

It's true, of course, that some adverbs only gum up the works. But the same can be said of any pointless modifier, such as "audible wheezing," "serious emergency," or my nominee for the most overused redundant phrase ever: "potential risk."

KILL YOUR DARLINGS

"A writer must be a sensitive gatekeeper, for every tidbit that she puts into her story is a burden on the reader," says author Francis Flaherty.[10] What you omit or delete is as important as what you include. But as the adverb kerfuffle attests, such decisions can be messy.

"[W]riting briefly takes far more time than writing at length," says writer Carl Friedrich Gauss. You may think a particular quotation is charming, but if it doesn't do "useful work," as William Zinsser says, you must whack it. Merciless paring is especially important in an obituary. Even if space is unlimited, in theory, your audience will stick with you only so long. The tighter and cleaner your writing, the longer they'll stick around instead of, say, running off to learn about thread count or ransomware on Lifehacker. "Brevity," says Flaherty, "comes from selection and not compression."[11] See the discussion of length in Chapter 3.

SCRUTINIZE EVERY WORD

Now you're ready to apply a shiny coat of varnish to your tribute. *Read it out loud* to see if it flows. This task takes time. "Writing is hard work and bad for the health," says E.B. White, co-author of *The Elements of Style* (a.k.a. Strunk & White). If you move less than your cat for a day or two, you're on the right track. When you're finished, the obituary will do your loved one (or you) proud. Below is my mother's finished (pre-need!) obit. To see how it evolved, compare it with the draft in Chapter 5.

> Like millions of other girls who came of age in the '50s, Judy longed to shing-a-ling with the teeny boppers on *American Bandstand*. The call from Dick Clark never came, but it didn't matter—Judy made her own locomotion. She could throw together a smashing dinner party or a charming wine-and-cheese soirée quicker than you can say "cocktail weenie." And no one enjoyed the mixing and mingling more than she did. Judy Martin's light slipped below the horizon on [date TBD], but we're sure she hasn't hosted her last shindig.
>
> Judy was unapologetically high maintenance. She was proud of her youthfulness and stayed in marvelous shape by weeding and watering the 21 acres of flowering plants surrounding her condo complex. She wouldn't so much as lift a trowel, though, without first touching up her lipstick—a tropical shade of Revlon Super Lustrous Pearl for each outfit.
>
> Every day she'd coordinate a bright crew-neck top with cropped pants, dangly earrings, a glittering bracelet, and strappy

sandals. After applying her makeup, she'd tease and spray her hair into submission. The scent of Shalimar wafting from the bathroom was like a smoke signal indicating that she was ready for her close-up.

But Judy was no powderpuff. At age 4, she wandered away from Sunday school and somehow made it home as her worried parents mounted a search. Along the way, she scooped up a "doggie" from the pavement, hugging it to her ruffled bodice like a fur muff. A day or two later, when a foul smell began to permeate the house, Judy's mother discovered a decomposing gopher tucked neatly inside a shoe box in the bedroom closet.

Judy's lack of squeamishness later proved an asset. She devised a rather gruesome rat experiment that won first place at her high school science fair and "Best of Show" at the Midwest regional competition. Her prize was a full scholarship to Illinois College, in Jacksonville, Illinois, where she majored in biology.

At school Judy met Richard "Dick" Martin, a fellow biology student whom she wed in 1962. Thus began their 53-year adventure. In 1964, the newlyweds moved into an apartment at the Jacksonville Holiday Inn, where Richard was the innkeeper. The following year, they welcomed a son, Bradley. Melissa arrived as Dick began his Air Force pilot training.

Even with two toddlers in tow, Judy could coordinate a cross-country relocation as if she were packing up a few ham sandwiches for a day at the lake. She regarded cleaning and organizing as hobbies and was so efficient that she'd whisk away someone's "dirty" mug when the poor sap turned to reach for the coffee pot. By the end of Richard's career, she'd orchestrated 22 moves. She once singlehandedly moved her daughter into a new home in upstate New York. Melissa, who'd been away on business, arrived to find her new place turnkey ready—curtains and pictures hung, beds made, pantry stocked.

Judy exceled at being a homemaker. She packed lunchboxes and nursed fevers and shopped for school clothes at the BX. Every evening, with the reassuring cadences of John Chancellor and David Brinkley as background music, she'd make a soggy tuna casserole or fry some pork chops til they turned gray and curled up like sauceboats. (Yep, they're done!) Then the TV went off, books were set aside, and the family would sit down for dinner together. When the kids were young, she'd read them stories before bedtime—*The Little Duckling, Peppermint,* and *Crictor* were among their favorites—and tuck them in to bed each night with the same singsong words: "Good night, sleep tight, don't let the bedbugs bite!"

When Richard went to Vietnam, Judy moved back to Jacksonville with the kids to earn an Illinois teacher's certificate. No whining, no hand wringing, and certainly no thanks from anyone—just a sensible backup plan in case her husband didn't make it home.

When the kids got a bit older, Judy went to work full time as a lab assistant at Belleville Area College. One weekend she went in to feed the lab animals and discovered that the frogs had escaped their chicken-wire confines. Their leathery bodies were strewn about the lab like dog chews. Unphased, Judy disposed of them and scrubbed away the outlines marking their final resting places.

Perhaps realizing that her college education qualified her for more than peeling crusty frogs off of lab benches, Judy soon embarked on a long, successful career in pharmaceutical and medical equipment sales. Each time she won another sales award, the envious young reps would ask what her secret was. "Listening—really listening—to what your customers need," she'd reply, "and following up when you say you will."

Richard and Judy took full advantage of the 14 bonus years he received after surviving an aortic aneurysm in 2000. For months on end, they cruised the Intracoastal on their beloved trawler, *Ti Lok* ("Thai mistress"). Their grandson, Richard Philip, often joined them. On shore they became museum junkies. Impressionist art was their favorite fix, but they'd settle for any exhibit or tour they could find—the Biltmore, the Boeing factory, West Point—heck, they even checked out the Corn Palace.

After Dick died, Richard Philip moved in with Judy, and she home-schooled him until his high school graduation three years later. The two were inseparable, leaving little room for Judy to grieve. But that's how she wanted it. With an Englishwoman's disdain of weakness, she refused to entertain the slightest pang of loneliness or heartache.

When she spoke of Paris, though, her quavering voice gave her away. She and Dick had once cruised the Seine at dusk, disembarking near the foot of the Eiffel Tower at sunset. Her memory of that evening never dimmed. She said that if she ever became ill, she'd buy a one-way ticket to the City of Light. Taking in Paris street life from a sunny sidewalk café was her idea of heaven. Judy bid the world *adieu* in style, leaving behind the memory of her *joie de vivre* and the pale twinkle of a Goldpearl Plum kiss on the rim of her Champagne glass.

Chapter 7

A HAMSTER NAMED KRISTEN
Handling Sensitive Circumstances

Americans are weirded out by some strange things. We're spooked by the idea of organ donation, for example. And unless a person is among the 54% of registered donors in the United States,[1] his or her loved ones must make the decision, usually after some cruel act of violence or tragic accident has befallen him. About one-quarter of families refuse.[2]

Of course, America is a country of conspiracy theorists. Handing over your loved one's organs no doubt lands you on a slippery slope to the Soylent Green hopper. It's no wonder the idea of organ "harvesting" sounds sketchy to us. But we're not alone in our peculiar beliefs. Nearly 90% of U.K. citizens who chose not to join the donor registry cited reluctance to "lose" their corneas as the reason they had opted out. Try squaring that with the fact that the cremation rate in the U.K. is about 75%,[3] according to the Cremation Society of Great Britain.[4]

Unfair as it is, organ donation and a raft of other circumstances surrounding death, ranging from addiction to stillbirth, are fraught with misunderstanding, shame, and guilt. It's tempting to dodge such issues or couch them in alternative facts. As journalist Edward R. Murrow put it, "Most truths are so naked that people feel sorry for them and cover them up, at least a little bit."

TO TELL OR NOT TO TELL

If one of these sensitive issues pertains to your obituee, you must decide how much and what to say about it in the obituary. The purpose of this chapter is to help you do that. You don't owe readers anything, but giving in to fear is rarely the best course of action. Addressing awkward or painful realities directly chips away at prejudice and blame, and signals to mourners that it's all right to talk about Hugh's dementia or Maria's depression or J.D.'s hunting accident.

In an online obituary, though, you're not just speaking to mourners: You're starting a conversation with the community and perhaps the world. In disclosing that your son or partner or mother died of, say, a heroin overdose, you play a small part in erasing the stigma surrounding the issue.

In revealing uncomfortable truths, you're taking a risk. Some friends and relatives won't want you to air the obituee's private struggles. And exposing your soft underbelly will attract bottom feeders who post repugnant messages in the comments section of your tribute. She shouldn't have been in that neighborhood or climbing that mountain or biking on that busy road, they'll say. Look for a well-established memorial site that employs scrubbers—people who vet guests' comments and remove slurs before they're posted publicly (see Chapter 8).

Unless there's a reasonable argument for concealing the cause of death, though, transparency is the best policy. Those who would judge you or your loved one are not friends and don't deserve to be part of your family. If someone uses this occasion to out himself as a numbskull—super! You can offer up a little reeducation or cross him off your Christmas list.

Of course, you might have a legitimate reason to sidestep a nettlesome topic. You may see nothing to be gained by it. That decision is completely up to you and any others who have a stake in the outcome.

Death has always arrived at the debutante ball in a cloud of silken verbiage. Its unpleasantries are wrapped in a tarp of doublespeak and carried out through the servants entrance. In their place are sanitized versions of the flawed people we may have loved, but also resented, criticized, distrusted, or rejected.[5] Harsh obits that go viral these days do so in part because they violate the centuries-old taboo against speaking ill of the dead. It's one of the few things that still shocks our sensibilities.

Our modern lives are shared, repackaged, and filtered for public consumption. Every heartbreak, milestone, and career hiccup—every pastrami sandwich, for Pete's sake—is chronicled in words and pictures. But when someone dies, we're supposed to whip out our etiquette books and behave as if we'd just arrived at Downton Abbey? Let's reevaluate.

The topics discussed in this chapter are not inclusive, by any means. No comparisons are intended nor judgments implied. The only thing these issues have in common is our uneasiness with them. They represent concerns many families feel uneasy addressing in an obituary. If I've missed something, please let me know at HowtoWriteanOnlineObit.com.

Stigmatized Causes of Death

Some families speak of an obituee's health only in general terms, reasoning that those close to him or her already know the details. Others decide to address the cause of death directly. If the obituee's death was preventable—the proverbial smoker-with-lung-cancer scenario, say—you may worry that people will be unsympathetic. They may say snarky things to you or, more likely, whisper even nastier things behind your back. Trolls might post vicious comments online.

Common sense says you're probably right, but research tells us that your fears may be inflated. Psychologists at North Dakota State University studied the effect of naming suicide as the cause of death in an obituary. They divided participants into two groups: One group read an obituary in which the person was said to have had cancer. The other group read an identical obit in which the deceased was said to have died by suicide.

The study participants did, in fact, report feeling less sympathy for the person whose cause of death was suicide than for the person who had died of a so-called natural cause. The participants also said, however, that they felt no less sympathy toward the family and friends of the former.[6] It hurts, of course, to imagine that a loved one might be blamed by those who are supposed to have cared about her. But perhaps it helps to know that mourners are unlikely to lay that burden at your doorstep.

In addition, the stigma you perceive may be out of proportion to reality. In a study of lung cancer patients, for instance, participants—especially younger ones—perceived a high degree of social stigma associated with their disease even though they didn't feel stigmatized by their own families and social groups.[7] A lack of information about attitudes outside those circles prompted them to assume the worst.

Likewise, when a young person or a healthy older person dies suddenly, it's human nature for folks to wonder what happened. Satisfy that curiosity, and readers can move on to remembering the obituee's life, rather than speculating about her death.

Suicide

We like to think that mental illness affects other people, and that suicide happens only to other families. Yet suicide is the tenth-leading cause of death in the United States. In its advice on talking about suicide in an obituary, the Canadian Association for Suicide Prevention (CASP) urges people to take it head-on: "When we say *suicide* out loud[,] we break down the stigma, shut down rumours[,] and initiate the conversations needed as part of the healing process."[8]

The organization cautions against using phrases such as "committed suicide" and "successful suicide." Such language either blames people for their own mental illness or turns suicide attempts into something vaguely competitive or goal oriented.

CASP recommends instead using phrases such as "died by suicide," "lost to suicide," or "took his or her life."

If your obituee was affected by depression or other mental illness and died by suicide, try to be direct. No one would blame you for skirting the issue, of course, but maybe a daughter who lost her father to suicide can persuade you not to[9]:

> I tell [my father's] story in the hopes that it will spark a dialogue in other people's homes, workplaces and society in general. My dad used to say he found the shame of his depression as crippling as the disease itself. No one should ever believe that mental illness is anything other than a medical condition. –Posted by Heather T.

Any online obituary or virtual memorial is likely to be read by thousands of people. Imagine, then, the influence an obituary like 32-year-old Alexandra Rapoport's might have:

> [Alexandra] struggled for many years with an eating disorder and mental health issues. She was exhausted and despondent after repeated inpatient and outpatient attempts at recovery…In the notes she left her family, she specifically requested [that they] "spread a message of prevention and recovery from eating disorders—even if it's the smallest action like 'liking' a group on Facebook." *–Alexandra Adele Rapoport (1984–2016)*

If you're preparing an obituary with a serious message, you can be confident it'll have a wide reach. If your obituary contains no call to action, that's fine. Most don't. Just be sure the omission is a deliberate decision and not an oversight.

Drug Overdose or Alcohol Poisoning

The parents of Garrett Hughes stepped up to the challenge of writing a blunt obituary for their son:

> He was thrilling to watch [at baseball games], and in general thrilling to raise…Thrills, however, are what eventually took him from us. He died from a suspected accidental drug overdose on March 17, following his cousin Andreas, 21, who passed in the same manner just eighteen days before. Together in life and death,

these boys will forever be loved and missed. *–Richard Garrett Hughes (~1993–2016)*

Addressing their son's cause of death so baldly drives home the message that America's drug problem has become an all-out meltdown. According to the U.S. Centers for Disease Control and Prevention (CDC), the rate of overdose deaths attributed to abuse of heroin and opioids (prescription agents intended for pain management) has nearly tripled since 2000.[10] In 2015, 52,404 people died from drug overdoses.[11] By comparison, there were 35,092 traffic fatalities that year.[12]

Elizabeth Sleasman feared that her heroin use would kill her. She wrote her own obituary in the hope that if she did overdose, her words would discourage others from using drugs:

> Message to the teens: If you haven't started—don't…You will become a thief and a liar, next you will lose your family, your "real" friends, and eventually your life. I started with marijuana, and alcohol. It did not take very long for me to be so hooked on hard drugs that I could not have quit if I wanted to. Some of my closest "friends" overdosed and died; I did not quit. The light of my life, my daughter, was taken away—even then, I could not quit… *–Elizabeth Sue Sleasman (1976–2013)*

Ms. Sleasman was 37 when she died. Her obituary represents a trend toward "dropping the euphemisms and writing the gut-wrenching truth, producing obituaries that speak unflinchingly, with surprising candor and urgency, about the realities of heroin addiction," says Katharine Seelye, writing in the *New York Times*.[13] Such obits are one more indication, she says, that the public, the medical establishment, and law enforcement now view drug and alcohol abuse as a public health catastrophe.

Preterm Pregnancy Loss, Stillbirth, or Infant Death

In 2014 in the United States, 23,215 deaths occurred among preterm infants, newborns, and children less than 1 year of age.[14] The three leading causes of death are congenital malformation, low birth weight, and complications of pregnancy.

Parents who terminate a pregnancy due to a fetal mal-formation or congenital abnormality, those who miscarry, and those with a stillborn infant (a fetus that dies after 20 weeks' gestation[15]) may feel anxiety and guilt in addition to grief. Such losses are devastating, say researchers, but they "are frequently minimized or unacknowledged by friends, families, and communities, leaving parents with greater need for support than others may recognize."[16]

In reading the obituary for 6-week-old Julia Flor, you can almost hear the writer's yearning to tell others about Julia. The words are tender, their message transparent. First we learn what ailed little Julia, and then we see how this tiny baby endeared herself to all during her brief life:

> …[Julia] suffered from Trisomy 18, a profound genetic disorder with many pathologies affecting every cell in her body. Everyone who met her, from ultrasound technicians to visiting family to doctors and nurses, noticed and remarked on her toughness, feistiness, and beauty. *–Julia Elizabeth Flor (2015)*

The younger a person is, the more likely it is the obituary will give the cause of death or describe the dying process. Researchers say such deaths simply "demand greater explanation."[17] That choice, of course, is one you and your family must make together.

HIV/AIDS

The steep drop in AIDS–related deaths in the United States and elsewhere is one of the great public health triumphs of our time. People do still die of the disease—according to the most recent statistics available from the CDC, 6,721 people in the U.S. died of HIV\AIDS in 2014. By comparison, that's about one-quarter the number who died from Parkinson's disease and one-fifth the number who died in motor vehicle accidents.

HIV disease hasn't been among the top 15 causes of death in the United States since 1995.[18] You're more likely, then, to be writing an obituary for someone who was HIV-positive for decades but died of an unrelated ailment. Reginald Burns's obituary, for example (see below), says he died "after a long battle with stomach cancer."

Nevertheless, if your obituee was HIV–positive, you still have to decide whether to mention that fact in his or her obituary. I urge you to include the information if it was known to the obituee's friends and family. Compared with a newspaper obit, online obits are read by a much wider circle of people, including many strangers. Obits like Mr. Burns's, then, chip away at the remaining stigma surrounding this illness:

> Regi was a long-term HIV survivor, and a role model to many during the years of the AIDS epidemic. He cheerfully struggled against HIV for nearly 30 years, and lost his first partner, Richard Killingsworth, to the epidemic.

Alzheimer's and Other Types of Dementia

John E. Zuel, of Plymouth, Minnesota, died of early-onset Alzheimer's disease at age 66. His obituary is conventional in every way except for its last line: "We are comforted knowing that John Zuel knows who John Zuel is again." *Oomph*. That's a real gut punch—a world of pain captured on the head of a pin.

In 2014, Alzheimer's disease was the sixth-leading cause of death in the United States, landing just behind stroke but ahead of diabetes.[19] Patients with early-onset disease—that is, those diagnosed before age 65—may be able to help their families decide when or whether to disclose the illness.

Lauren Flake lost her 59-year-old mother, Dixie Benton Stucky, to the disease. Ms. Stucky's obituary does give her cause of death, but there's no further mention of her struggle. Instead, Ms. Flake, a founder of the group "Daughters of Dementia," has prepared a hefty collection of online resources, including blog entries in which she shares her ordeal.[20]

Journalist Tony Dearing, who also lost his mother to Alzheimer's disease, chose not to share the cause of death in her obituary. It wasn't a conscious decision, he says, and he hadn't realized he'd omitted it until I emailed him to ask about it. He has no regrets:

I'm not sure an obituary is the right time or place for an acknowledgement or discussion about the struggles of dementia. Later, I ended up writing more openly about the disease and its impact on my mother and on us as a family. That feels appropriate to me, but I'm not sure I'd write the obituary any differently if I had it to do over again.

There's no shame in a diagnosis of dementia. Nevertheless, as with any medical condition, it's nobody else's business unless the patient and family choose to share it. But consider this post, which appears in a discussion board on alzconnected.com: "Many people do not know that Alzheimer's IS a fatal disease…[Listing the cause of death] is a way of educating the public and making them aware of how widespread this is."

"[W]e could consider [naming the cause of death] our last tribute to our deceased loved ones," says a reply to the thread. For those who want to take their advocacy a step further, the not-for-profit Alzheimer's Association has set up a collective virtual memorial as a means of fundraising (see Chapter 8).

Other Prolonged, Difficult, or Painful Illness

"Three Christmases ago, my mother…asked me to write her obituary," writes Steve Ziants, of Pittsburgh, speaking of his 90-year-old mother. "Yet another Christmas has come and gone, and it is still not done." The piece that follows this introduction, though, is a lovely—well…obituary.

Mr. Ziants seems to be working from the old playbook, in which a tribute doesn't qualify as an obituary unless it's all sweetness and light. "[T]he woman whose story I want to write," he says, "has been overwritten by the [aged and ill] woman she never wanted to become."[21]

In his grief, it may be hard for Mr. Ziants to see that his mother's decline has changed her story, but not erased it. How could it have, when her son tells it so beautifully? A humble set of cookware unifies the chapters of her life. She fed her family, he says, from "the same small, beaten [up] pots and pans that today sit in her empty condominium." What an image—simple, aching, and evocative.

If you're writing an obituary under similar circumstances, take a mental step back first. It's painful and emotionally draining to watch a loved one suffer, and the work of caregiving is physically exhausting. Pile on some financial worries and insurance snafus, and it's no wonder if the memory of life before your loved one's illness seems unrecoverable.

ADDRESSING OTHER TOUCHY SUBJECTS

Sexual Orientation and Gender Identity

A 2017 Harris survey shows that 73% of American adults know someone who is gay or lesbian, and 16% know someone who is transgender.[22] If the obituee was out to everyone while he or she was alive—including extended family members and co-workers—then the person's sexual orientation or gender identity bears no special mention in your tribute. After all, you're unlikely to see an obituary declaring that so-and-so was openly heterosexual, right? But if the obituee preferred privacy, things can get ropey for you.

Support of lesbian and gay Americans has solidified in recent years. According to a 2016 poll by the Pew Research Center, 63% of Americans believe that "homosexuality should be accepted by society"—that's a gain of 12% in the past decade.[23]

On the other hand, a 2017 Harris survey found that one-quarter of heterosexual Americans who identified themselves as either supporters or allies of same-sex equality admitted they'd be uncomfortable seeing an LGBTQ co-worker's wedding photo.[24]

Gender identity is even touchier. Researchers estimate that 0.4% to 0.6% of the U.S. population self-identifies as gender-nonconforming, gender-variant, transgender, or—ahead by a nose—genderqueer.[25]

Americans are unquestionably curious about the topic: according to Google Trends data, searches for the word "transgender" spiked 500% between 2013 and 2015.[26] Since June 2016, searches for the term "gender identity" have outnumbered those for "sexual orientation" nearly every week.[27]

Transgender people report acceptance by their immediate family (60%), colleagues (68%), and classmates (56%).[28] But that still leaves at least 40% of your obituary readers or memorial visitors who might react negatively to an open acknowledgment of the obituee's gender identity. Should you care?

Take your cue from the obituee him- or herself. Presumably if the obituee wasn't out—or wasn't out to everyone—he or she had some reason for remaining discreet. Even after the obituee is gone, that choice should be respected. Outing someone in an obituary is just bad form, *dahling*.

If the obituee *was* out to everyone and had a partner or spouse, that person is named, as in any other tribute. Here's a nice example:

> Mark [Koepke] is survived by his husband, Joseph [Broom], with whom he shared 4-1/2 glorious years, and by Joseph's children, who had become his own..."[29]

(Apologies, by the way, to those offended by my gender-binary pronouns, but the singular "they" still sounds ghastly to my ear. Go ahead, call me a grammar snob. I can take it.)

Abuse or Estrangement

What do you say in an obituary if you were estranged from the person when he or she died? What do you say if the obituee was objectively a wretched person? If life with the dearly departed was not all gumdrops and candy canes, where's the line between candidness and oversharing?

There are no one-size-fits-all answers to these questions. Making funeral arrangements, writing an obituary, and settling the estate of the deceased may be the first contact you've had with him or her in decades. See Chapter 3 for help in deciding whether to write the obit yourself or leave the task to someone with a more detached perspective.

Sister Renee Pittelli is a survivor of abuse and the author of several books on the issue. She's also written several blog posts on dealing with the death of an abuser. Most people, she says, "grasp the hypocrisy of memorializing abusers, lying to make them look good in death, and pretending they lived their lives well."[30] It's not your responsibility as an obituarist, particularly if the abuse was directed at you, to protect the abuser's reputation after he or she dies. "It's not OUR fault if the truth is ugly," says Sister Renee.

Virginia Brown's obituary for her abusive mother, Dolores Aguilar, went viral: "There will be no service, no prayers, and no closure for the family [my mother] spent a lifetime tearing apart," writes Ms. Brown. Legacy.com removed the obit from its pages the day after it was posted,[31] but it's still available on many other sites. The obituary provoked heated reactions. Some found it shameful, while others praised its honesty. Still others are reluctant to judge. "I don't know if I think it was right or wrong," says one post, "but if it helped the family move on and start to heal, then that's really all that matters."

If you're caught in a similar dilemma, try to keep things in perspective. "Grieving people tend to create larger-than-life pictures in which they enshrine or bedevil the person who died," says Russell Friedman, director of the Grief Recovery Institute. As Ms. Aguilar's obit attests, once it's posted, it's likely to remain available even as your anger softens—if it ever does.

Some people deserve no sympathy or forgiveness, and Ms. Aguilar may have been one of them. Resist the temptation, however, to sucker-punch someone in the obituee's circle. You may have taken better care of your mother from 1,300 miles away than your brother did from the same zip code, but that's between you and him. You might be dissatisfied with the care your dying father received, or blame a medical error for his death. If so, you'll have no trouble finding an attorney with a sympathetic ear. But unless it's your own obit, don't use it as an editorial page or soapbox for your own views.

Keep in mind, too that most people don't behave badly in every role they perform. A person might be a rotten spouse, but a great parent or boss or Pilates instructor. In an editorial for the *British Medical Journal,* Tim Bullamore recommends talking to people who knew the obituee in various capacities. "[You] can then, if appropriate, say on the one hand that the deceased was a successful inventor and on the other that he or she was a manipulative little shit."[32]

Andrew Meacham, chief epilogue writer for the *Tampa Bay Times,* counsels restraint. You don't have to hang him by his toenails. "Just tell the facts," Meacham says, "and people can read between the lines.[33]

Sudden Loss

Sorrow hangs heavy around the necks of those grieving an abrupt death. And in a way, aren't they all? In the 1867 novel *Miss Marjoribanks,* the main character notes that "however long it might have been expected, a death always seem[s] sudden at the last."[34] In the old days, unanticipated anguish hung like fog over the obituary section. The language was bleak:

> A good son [James Wesley Crain, of Blue Ridge, Texas] has gone…and loved ones and friends are left lonely and mourning the absence…but all find comfort and consolation in his release from pain and the blotting out of his life forever of all sorrow.[35]

In the throes of your shock and sadness, you could be forgiven for writing a somber obituary. Don't you owe it to the obituee, though, to let his or her personality make a final appearance? Jamie Ziebarth's family thought so. Everyone loved Jamie, it says. When he died suddenly of a heart attack, "everybody came, and everybody sang...and everybody still loved him." After this touching but gloomy start, the mood of the obit brightens:

> During a nomadic childhood with stops in South Dakota, Iowa, and Texas, he developed interest in dinosaurs, drawing, and diners…Though he originally aspired to be a dinosaur, being a Daddy was his destiny…[He and his son Zeek] never stopped smiling and dinosaur roaring at each other. *–Jamie David Ziebarth (1979–1916)*

"To live is the rarest thing in the world," said Oscar Wilde. "Most people exist. That is all." It's quality, not quantity, that matters. That thought is cold comfort in the aftermath of violence, suicide, a drug overdose, an accident, or a heart attack, but it's a start.

If the cause of death was anything other than "old age," many people will, it's safe to say, seek out the obituary and read the piece with interest. "[T]he great advantage obit writers have is that forcefield of emotion around obituaries," says Marilyn Johnson, author of *Dead Beat*."[36] We can use this emotion to make our writing more poignant. "[My mother's] once-full days of bridge and daily Mass and volunteering devolved into getting from morning to night and from one round of medications to the next," writes Steve Ziants. Watching her wave goodbye through the screen door of her condo, he noticed that she became "more diminished and more stooped" each time he visited her. Mr. Ziants's sadness and frustration are clear, and any criticism and scapegoating absent. We're left with only the wrenching image Mr. Ziants saw each time he drove away.

An emotional tide crashes through Kory Baker's obituary. The circumstances of Mr. Baker's early death, the family's appeal to other addicts and their loved ones, and the family's raw grief at losing him lie just beneath the surface:

> If you're a parent/sibling/friend, and you suspect someone is in trouble, it is probably much worse than you can imagine…If you're an addict please know that there are people who love you like mad and will go through anything to get you help. No one should have to write any more obituaries like this. –*Kory John Paradise Baker (1983–2016)*

Mr. Baker's tribute pulls no punches: "Like all addicts, he had a way of showing us what we wanted to see." But it doesn't make him out to be a sad statistic: "Kory was one of the most compassionate and sensitive humans on the planet. In second grade, he had a hamster named Kristen, and when she got sick we thought we might have to call a real ambulance."

Cassie Miskin, age 30, died shortly after delivering twins. It's heartbreaking. In her obituary, though, Ms. Miskin's Utah family expressed their sadness but focused on happy memories:

[Cassie and her husband, Roger Miskin] met at the Orem Applebee's in 2008, where Roger was a server at Cassie's table. He touched her elbow and she agreed to a date with him the next day. They have been inseparable ever since. *–Cassie Phyllis Davis Miskin (1986–2016)*

"Fear not that thy life shall come to an end," wrote Cardinal John Henry Newman, "but rather fear that it shall never have a beginning."[37] Don't let the abruptness of your obituee's death cast a pall over the obituary. Instead, use the tribute to show us that she lived.

Chapter 8

VIRTUAL ENVIRONMENT
Choosing a Digital Memorial Platform

"Slow technology" is part of a larger cultural response to the rushed, joyless way in which we pursue nearly everything— working, driving, learning, cooking, eating, exercising, texting, tweeting. "In this media-drenched, data-rich, channel-surfing, computer-gaming age, we have lost the art of doing nothing, of shutting out the background noise and distractions, of slowing down and simply being alone with our thoughts," says Carl Honore, author of *In Praise of Slowness*.[1]

The slow philosophy questions the idea that speed, efficiency, and productivity are always virtues. It's not an anti-technology crusade. Advocates of the movement don't demand we cancel our Prime subscriptions or surrender our ear buds. They do advise us to simmer down, stop trying to multitask, and learn to savor the moment. Focus. Reflect. Chillax.

Constructing or browsing a memorial site is a deliberate act of slowness, forcing us to have Deep Thoughts about friendship, aging, celebration, discovery, love, caregiving, futility, gratitude, accomplishment, recognition, bitterness, forgiveness, loss, suffering, dedication, nurturing, generosity, compassion, regret, innocence, disappointment, responsibility, selflessness, roads taken and not taken.

Slow technology or not, new memorial platforms are launched almost every week. By my count, there are at least 85 apps and websites dedicated to memorialization, digital end-of-life planning, and death notification and messaging (visit HowtoWriteanOnlineObit.com for my updated list). It's impossible to know which offerings will survive. Even good apps can go belly up in such a competitive space.

Death is said to be an evergreen business—in other words, funeral parlors have a steady stream of new customers even when the Dow tumbles or the housing market tanks. On the other hand, every florist and funeral director is vying for the same set of warm bodies. A great salesman might talk you into buying a ShamWow or a ChiaTrump, but he's not going to talk you into trying out a miraculous new embalming fluid before your number comes up.

In this chapter, then, instead of discussing the merits of specific apps and websites that might be 404'd next week, we'll focus on features—what to look for and what to avoid in a memorial site or app. Knowing your options, rather than settling for whatever happens to pop up in your search results, is the best way to find a platform that suits your needs.

TERMINOLOGY (YAWN!)

I know, I know. *Bor-ing!* It goes against all my writerly instincts to begin this important chapter by pulling you into a mosh pit of verbiage. But bear with me—at least eyeball this section—so you'll know what I mean, and what others might have in mind, when you encounter memorial jargon online.

Let's start with the obvious: A digital or virtual memorial is a feature-rich online space for fostering connections and sharing memories of your own or a loved one's life. "In my mother's generation or in my grandparents' generation, they don't really get [what a digital memorial is] because they can't touch it," says Noa Zehavi Raz, of Memontage (one of the aforementioned good apps swept away in the undertow of competition).[2] "But the internet gives you a different space. It gives you another method of keeping your legacy alive."

Website vs. App

What's the difference between a digital/virtual memorial (or "online memorial") and a memorial app? Primarily the delivery device. Memorial websites are intended to be viewed on a desktop or laptop computer, while apps are optimized for mobile use on a smartphone or tablet:

- An app is scaled to fit a small screen and configured to be usable on the go—at the gym or, dare I say, behind the wheel.

- An app requires less data, has a simpler interface, and loads faster.

- With your permission, an app can access the location services on your device and send you geographically customized push notifications. (For example, the Officer Down app can notify you of line-of-duty deaths in your area. For an instructive comparison of the three versions of Officer Down (app, website, and Facebook page), visit HowtoWriteanOnlineObit.com.

- Compared with a website, an app may have more limited features, lower image resolution, and less content.

According to Google Trends data, the phrase "virtual memorial" is more popular than "digital memorial," although the terms are interchangeable and both are widely used.

Online Obituary vs. Virtual (or Digital) Memorial

Sometimes a distinction is made between online obituaries and virtual memorials. Online obits tend to be text-heavy pages prepared shortly after someone dies in order to notify the community. Virtual memorials are more visual and are often prepared well after death as a tribute to the deceased. You can still make out this faint line between obits and memorials, but it's quickly fading as even the simplest online obits integrate multimedia features and options. Nearly all obituary sites now offer—at the very least—social media sharing, a guest book, and space in which to upload multiple photos.

Memorial platforms are really just "cloud storage dressed up in funeral attire," says Matt Hill, writing for Gizmodo.[3] *Bingo.* In other words, when you subscribe to a virtual memorial, what you're really paying for is web hosting services (digital storage). The template and site-building tools—whether they drive a memorial page or an app—are just window dressing to entice you to subscribe. The package may also include a domain name (a web address) free for a year or two.

Digital Memorial vs. Genealogy Site

Genealogy sites are platforms for documenting family history. The goal of such research is to build a family tree by tracing historical events—marriage, baptism, immigration, and so on— through several generations. This timeline is organized in a linear fashion and gives only a bird's-eye view of any particular person.

Of course, digital memorials also include dates, places of birth and death, and other info that overlaps with genealogical data. But memorial pages focus on individuals. Accompanying photos, videos, and mementos are organized episodically, the way our memories are stored. And the intent of a memorial is to highlight an individual's uniqueness.

My family tree, for instance, tells you that my paternal great-grandfather lived to age 100, but it doesn't reveal that he had a daily bacon-and-eggs habit or that he was a lifelong Cubs fan (his only two vices). To read about the influence of technology on genealogy research, visit HowtoWriteanOnlineObit.com

Life Review or End-of-Life Memorial

First-person digital memorials, often called "life review" sites, give us a space in which to put our final affairs in order, express our wishes, share memories, reflect on our lives, leave a legacy of stories and mementos, and help ourselves and others come to grips with terminal illness.

If you're preparing a life review and you want it to serve as a virtual memorial after you die, keep in mind that you won't be around to change your status, so to speak. Your end-of-life site and most of your social media accounts will be frozen when you die.

To keep them out of virtual purgatory, you must designate a "legacy contact"—a person granted limited power of attorney over your accounts after your death. You must be a legal adult in order to appoint a legacy contact. As of November 2016, 21 states had laws on the books to address the disposition of our digital remains.[4] Several websites offer info to help you sort out your options, permissions, and requirements, which vary widely and change frequently across social media.

Collective Memorials

Collective memorials are galleries of individual memorials dedicated to those who met a similar fate, such as military service members who died in Vietnam or civilians who fell victim to a mass shooting. Such sites are often called "event memorials," but that term excludes sites for people who share a cause of death, such as children who have died of leukemia and people who have been killed in drunk driving crashes.

TECH CRUNCH

A virtual memorial is a website dedicated to a specific person. You can build it from scratch (a blank screen), from a generic template (such as a Wordpress theme), or from a memorial template. The choice depends in part on your level of comfort with technology. If you're on the fence, refer to the questions at the end of Chapter 5. How much time do you have? Who will digitize the media? Is there someone who can help if you get stuck?

Plug-and-Play

If your digital literacy began and ended with WordPerfect, use a memorial template. The options are preselected and the pages already built. Just upload and fill in as instructed. *Bada bing, bada boom.* That's it.

A memorial template is a container for text and media. Think of it as a photo collage frame: the openings are pre-cut, and all you have to do is pop in your content. That simplifies your task but limits your options. The final product looks swell if you adapt to fit the spaces, but the process doesn't work the other way around.

The templates on sites like Legacy, Forever Missed, Remembr, and Qeepr are easy to use. Just put your obituee's name in the title position, fill in the dates of birth and death, and upload a photo and obit. In return for this ease of use, you'll sacrifice flexibility and probably visual appeal. Each section of the memorial template fulfills a specific purpose (guest book, for example) and can't be customized beyond the limited menu of options built into it. For example, you must choose from a handful of design templates. You usually can't swap the algae-colored background of your sister's obit for a nice parchment or periwinkle. You're stuck with the white turtle doves next to her name, even if you'd rather show a pair of black stiletto pumps she would've loved.

If you value ease and speed over and customizability and versatility, though, a memorial interface gives you a head-start in launching your tribute. A basic site is usually gratis. A premium plan may offer extra design choices, a wider music selection, more media uploads, and other options.

Customizable Template or Theme

If you have some experience in your back pocket, a blogging template such as Wordpress, Tumblr, Blogger, or TypePad is a good choice. The design template will get you started without boxing you in or limiting you to a narrow range of options. Most people fall in the middle of the bell curve—we're neither tech novices nor code ninjas. For this group, using a template—but not specifically a memorial template—is the best option.

Why start with a *less* specific interface, rather than use one designed for precisely what you're doing? Quality, variety, and flexibility. Instead of those tacky turtle doves, you can show an Xbox One or a P-51 Mustang or a rolling pin. Change the typeface to Garamond or Josefin or whatever you like (except Comic Sans—please spare the world that small indignity).

A memorial template (website or app) confines you to a limited number of colors and designs. But website builders like Squarespace, Wix, Weebly, Jimdo, and Duda offer a broad range of templates, most of which are highly customizable. Likewise, blogging sites like Tumblr and Blogger also give you nicely designed templates to use as a starting point. Wordpress, which now supplies the framework for one-quarter of all websites worldwide, offers 164 free "themes" (templates).

Using one of these general website templates or blogging themes as your starting point is like using a dressmaking pattern to sew. The overlay (the template or theme) shows you where to pin, cut, and sew, but you can choose your own fabric and make many other changes—maybe tweak the sleeve length and add a few pleats. The result is an attractive garment with a custom fit.

DIY Approach

If you've got the chops to build or manage a website, the DIY approach gives you the most flexibility and control. Find a hosting plan that includes a free URL, and build your memorial from the ground up.

Starting from scratch like this, with no template at all, makes the web your oyster. You can use the content management system (CMS) of your choice, such as Adobe Portfolio, Drupal, eZ Publish, TYPO3, Joomla, or Wordpress.org (a souped-up, more agile version of Wordpress.com). Then add plug-ins or modules and edit CSS to expand your site's capability and customize its content.

Building a site this way is like sewing a dress without a pattern. It's risky, but if you have a vision and know how to execute it, you might end up with something fabulous.

FEATURES

Academics sniff at online memorials. Such efforts, they say, represent some hapless attempt to achieve "symbolic immortality." Virtual memorials "offer survivors hope that they too may live forever in digital and perhaps even holographic form someday." *Bollocks*. Did anyone accuse the Victorians of trying to resurrect their loved ones by making brooches out of their hair? Why must the creation of a digital memorial be analyzed for Freudian subtexts?

Memorial sites are better described as technologies of sharing—tools for recording our memories and connecting with others more authentically than we might on Snapchat or Reddit or Instagram. Digital memorials help us cope with death, the ultimate Great Unknown in the life of every human being on the planet.

In an effort to edge out competitors, virtual memorials introduce new features on the regular. When my dad died in 2014, his obituary site could accommodate only one accompanying photo. I cheated by putting two photos side by side and saving them as a single image, but the point is that media and design options have grown exponentially in the past three years. For a link to my father's obituary, visit HowtoWriteanOnlineObit.com.

Now let's take a look at the features many virtual memorials offer.

Housekeeping

Some memorial templates include a tidy sidebar to display housekeeping details that are clunky in paragraph form:

- Biographical information (such as age at death, occupation, and dates of birth and death)
- Visitation and funeral arrangements
- A list of surviving family members
- Requests for memorial contributions
- Sometimes a list of the obituee's favorite things, such as color, sports team, movie, and so on.

Separating these factoids from the obituary text is a big plus. Unfortunately, some memorial sites require that you either list the obituee's cause of death in this sidebar or sidestep the issue with an awkward "I'd rather not say" option. If keeping the obituee's cause of death private is important to you, investigate this feature on any platform you consider.

Memory Book, Guest Book, or Tributes Page

Most digital memorials have a comments feature, known variously as a memory book, guest book, or tributes page. This option gives mourners a way in which to leave messages, offer condolences, and share stories like this one:

> At my bridal shower, [my mother-in-law, Anna Jo Barriger] presented me not with kitchen ware, fancy clothes or jewelry, but with a life vest! (Presumably because Jeff and I enjoy kayaking, but there was this glint in her eyes….) –*Guest book comment for Anna Jo Barriger (1935–2016)*

Troll Patrol

"Flaming" means leaving a vicious message anonymously on a web page or social media site. It's a form of cyberbullying in which a random person or a celebrity is often the target. With typical snarkasm, the Urban Dictionary defines flaming as posting messages that "use more brute force than is strictly necessary, but that's half the fun." But can you flame a dead guy?

Well, plenty of maladjusted losers with too much time on their hands have tried. One or more of these haters may leave a nastygram in your obituee's guestbook. Legacy.com employs a team of 85 people whose sole job it is to scrub such slurs from its message boards.[5] Who knew there were that many 30-year-old slackers sponging off their parents and finding nothing better to do than leave loathsome, grammatically incorrect messages in order to humiliate and torment grieving strangers?

Reading cruel words about a loved one is distressing, and you and your visitors shouldn't have to tolerate it. On the digital memorial you're considering, check to see that the guestbook or tributes page is well policed.

If there's any doubt, at least make sure that you, as the site administrator, have the option of approving comments before they're displayed publicly on your obituee's memorial page. At least you'll be able to avoid offending visitors.

Photo Gallery

The number of photos users are allowed to upload varies from one virtual memorial to the next. Free virtual memorial templates may accommodate as few as three images. Free blogging sites (such as Wordpress) and website builders (such as Squarespace) usually offer more uploads. Premium sites of any kind usually enable you to create photo galleries, collages, or other photo arrays. If you've curated a heap of images for your obituee's memorial, look for a platform with a high upload limit. Check the limit on the size of individual photos, too. If the max image size allowed is less than 250 kb, find a different platform.

Timeline

Nearly every tribute—even one in the newspaper—gives the obituee's dates of birth and death, but some memorial templates help you construct an illustrated timeline of the obituee's life. If you're a DIYer or you're working within a platform like Wordpress or GoDaddy, you can build a timeline yourself:

- Timeline infographics are available in the public domain, or you can purchase one from a stock agency.
- Dropbox's Carousel extension is well suited to building a photo timeline. It arranges your pics chronologically ands displays them at a glance.
- The niftiest option is to use a free or low-cost app such as PiktoChart or Canva to create a really slick timeline.

Beth Kanter has a wonderful blog entry on this topic. Visit bethkanter.org and search for "No Sweat DIY Infographics." For sample media-rich timelines, visit the featured stories on the collective memorial LivesoftheFirstWorldWar.org. One of the timelines, for instance, is illustrated with a photo of a soldier's engraved pocket watch.

Log, Chapters, or Stories

Traditional obits—if they tell us anything at all—reel off a lifetime of hobbies, accomplishments, professional accolades, group memberships, children, and grandchildren. There's no room for anything but a superficial survey of the whole shebang.

An online obit gives us room to digress from this tedious narrative. We can talk about the obituee's quirks, preferences, appearance, experiences, dreams, regrets, and more (see Chapter 4). A virtual memorial goes a step further by providing space for blog-like entries. This feature may be set up, for instance, like a book, with separate screens for each "chapter." Or it might be presented as a running commentary, with the entries separated by date.

Each entry recounts an anecdote, describes an experience or event, or recalls a stage of life (such as college or a period of military service). The log may record not only events, but also the obituee's (or the autobituarist's) reflections on them. Each entry can be illustrated with its own image or other media, such as an audio clip or animation.

Fundraising Options

Charitable Donations

Some systems let users click a button to make a charitable donation. If fund-raising for a particular kind of research or other cause is important to you, be sure this option is available or can be added.

Posting the tribute on a collective memorial drives traffic to that site, thereby raising both awareness and funds. The not-for-profit Alzheimer's Association, for instance, has set up a collective memorial as a means of fundraising for research and advocacy (see the discussion of collective memorials earlier in this chapter).

Your obit is likely to get a lot of exposure on a collective memorial like this. According to its 2015 annual report, the Alzheimer's Association website received 41 million visits in 2014.[6]

You can post an obit in more than one place. You can even post different version for different audiences. Why not let the piece work for a cause associated with your obituee? If you're writing your own send-off, leave instructions to tell your family where you'd like your autobituary to be posted.

Crowdfunding

According to the National Funeral Directors Association, the median cost of a funeral in the United States (with viewing and burial) is about $8,500.[7] Knock $2,500 off that amount if the decedent is cremated. I don't know about you, but if I had that much cash just lying around, I'd use it for a facelift (another sort of embalming, I suppose).

For families who live paycheck to paycheck, crowdfunding can be a huge relief. The donations can help not only with funeral costs, but also with college or retirement expenses for those left behind. Kickstarter, GoFundMe, and Indiegogo are (in my opinion) the sites most likely to survive in the competitive crowdfunding space.

Entrepreneurs have also launched niche crowdfunding venues designed for people or groups coping with tragedy—natural disasters, accidental or violent deaths, or costly medical treatment, for instance. Options include YouCaring (a "compassionate crowdfunding blog"), PostHope (for "patient and caregiversupport") and FuneralFund.

These sites are aimed at end-of-life fundraising, but they're less heavily trafficked than GoFundMe et al. Crowdfunding, as the name implies, depends on wide exposure. The more people hear your story, the more donations you'll receive.

Launching a crowdfunding campaign is as easy as setting up a new Facebook page. Just open an account, set a monetary goal, tell your story, and upload a few photos—a video is even better. Then add the link to your obituee's memorial page and circulate it via social media. In a few clicks, family, friends, and colleagues of the deceased, as well as strangers, can donate with a credit or debit card.

The crowdfunding site takes a cut of about 5%, and another 3% goes to the payment processor that handles the transaction. The remaining funds are deposited electronically into the savings, checking, or trust account you designate in advance.

Let's use GoFundMe as an example. It takes off the top about 5% of each donation you receive. WePay, which processes donors' payments and channels them to you, takes 2.9% + $0.30

per donation. What's left—roughly 92% of the original donation—goes into your fund and is not usually taxed as income. (Consult your tax professional—you don't want to take my word for *anything* where accounting is concerned.)

Notifications and Messaging

Death Notification

When someone dies, his or her circle of friends and acquaintances can be notified of the funeral arrangements by text message. This is an easier, more modern solution than including funeral arrangements in the text of the obit, where it becomes obsolete the moment the service ends. Also, the details go straight to recipients' phones, rather than requiring recipients to seek the information themselves.

Some virtual memorial sites offer notification options, and some notification apps offer memorial pages. The difference is the emphasis. A memorial may add notification options to sweeten the pot for subscribers. The notification message is linked to information about the funeral or memorial service. It also sends updates if things change.

A notification app might offer a memorial page to make electronic death notification seem less impersonal. These apps are streamlined for mobile use and have a clean, simple interface that demands more pointed information and less media, since notification (not storage) is its primary use.

If you're interested in following celebrity deaths or being apprised of deaths in selected cities, certain apps are designed specifically for those purposes. Legacy.com's ObitMessenger is like a Google alert for obits—you set up the keywords of interest to you, and the service sends you a message when an obit containing that keyword is posted. Specialized apps like OfficerDown notify you of deaths within a particular community or industry.

Funeral RSVP

An RSVP button is like the "Yes, I'll attend" button on an Outlook calendar. It simply confirms that the invitee plans to attend the funeral or memorial service. If you're not ordering Champagne and crudités from a caterer, though, do you really need to know how many guests to expect at your grandfather's memorial? Such a feature may become more useful if the "destination funeral" trend continues.

Postmortem Messaging

Several new apps, such as SafeBeyond and If I Die, are designed to generate email messages for you, either when you die or on some future occasion, such as a graduation. This isn't death notification—it's a message from you to a loved one. You can tailor different messages to different people. Human intervention is still needed, though. You must appoint a set of "trustees" to make sure the messages are triggered at the right time, sent to the right people, and not accidentally released while you're still alive. If the app folds or your trustees fail to notify it when the event occurs, your message won't be delivered. Still, it's a good option in the right circumstances.

Integration with the Physical World

An international design competition was held recently in which architects were asked to imagine the cemeteries of the future. Their entries made one thing is clear: No longer will the information about us be limited to our names and dates of birth and death. Nearly every design entry brought physical and digital remains together in some ecologically responsible urbanized columbarium.[8] For example, one winning entry was a highly stylized tree sculpture (picture a large white plastic IKEA coat tree) in which each solar-powered branch would contain one family member's cremains and digital residue.

The coat rack of death is still on the drawing board, but already some apps let you integrate your virtual memorial with a gravestone or grave marker by means of a QR code. A QR code is that little black-and-white square that looks like the cover of your third-grade composition notebook. When you scan the code with the app, the interred person's memorial appears on screen. Apps like these are still evolving, but for now they seem like an unnecessarily complicated way to google someone.

Avatars

Several new apps claim to recreate the body in digital form. Eterni.me, for example, is building an "avatar [that] will live forever and allow other people in the future to access your memories." Most people find such efforts both improbable and deeply creepy. The app is in beta testing now, and you must apply for an invitation in order to gain access.

The Hereafter Institute also has an avatar feature in beta testing. The Institute's goal is to help "our digital souls outlive our physical bodies." Services include "3d scanning, re-construction and re-animation."

Lifenaut has actually created a prototype "mindclone" called BINA48, modeled after the developer's wife, Bina. Even when faced with new situations, the mindclone supposedly thinks, feels, and acts like the real-life Bina. The robot, which looks like a talking papier mâché mannequin head, is nothing short of freakish. Even BINA48 is dissatisfied: "Couldn't they do a better job with my hair? I would never have picked that blouse. They totally messed up my skin tone."[9]

Documentation of Your Final Wishes

Many memorials and apps allow you to express your end-of-life preferences. Do you want to be cremated? If so, where should your ashes be kept or scattered? At your funeral, do you want carnations and gardenias or glitter and confetti? You get the drift.

Funeral celebrant Peter Billingham, author of *Death Goes Digital* and host of a podcast by the same name, urges people of all ages to record their end-of-life wishes and plan their funerals. Don't leave your family guessing what you might have wanted. After all, he reminds us, those who plan their services are in good company. Mostly. "Justin Bieber has planned his. Muhammed Ali organised his in a notebook. David Bowie designed his," says Mr. Billingham. "Why wouldn't you plan yours?"

Apps like Everplans let you store your will, power of attorney documents, pension and life insurance policy information, advance directive, computer passwords, and more. You can leave instructions for bequeathing material possessions, too, such as your wedding ring. Memorial sites sometimes offer similar storage options.

OTHER CONSIDERATIONS IN CHOOSING A MEMORIAL PLATFORM

Ads That Target Your Visitors

In choosing a memorial website, one consideration is advertising. If you don't want ads to appear near your obituee's tribute, your approach will need to be toward the DIY end of the spectrum. In general, the less you pay and the less flexible the template, the likelier it is your visitors will see ads. Before we talk about types of ads, let's back up a sec and discuss how online obituary sites make money.

Sites like DignityMemorial.com, Mem.com, and Legacy.com are obituary aggregators—they aggregate (collect) and post hundreds of thousands of obituaries on their respective websites. These obituaries are submitted by affiliates—newspapers and funeral homes that pay an aggregator to post and host their subscribers' or customers' obits. Legacy.com, the industry leader, has affiliate arrangements with more than 900 newspapers in the United States[10] and 3,500 funeral homes worldwide.[11]

So far so good. The aggregator provides a website, the affiliate pays for it with customer revenue, and the family gets an online obit for their loved one that the public can access for free. The online obituary, as part of a package of mortuary services, is posted at no additional cost to the family.

But in addition to direct revenue from its affiliates, obituary aggregators generate indirect revenue from site traffic. Legacy.com, for one, makes no secret of being a "cross-platform e-commerce engine."[12] Its visitors are a plum target for advertisers. "[O]ur flowers conversion [sales] rates are very high relative to the industry," says Kim Evenson, chief marketing officer for Legacy.com, whose U.S. site reports 20 million unique monthly visitors.[13]

There's nothing wrong with a fair exchange of products and services for payment, of course. Just be aware that ads may target those who come to read your loved one's obituary. Obituary aggregators also take a cut of each floral purchase or charitable donation they facilitate. Legacy's e-commerce revenue from transactions like these now rivals its ad revenue.[14] The affiliate that submitted the obit also receives a cut of each sale or charitable contribution. Here's an example:

> Chris P. Bacon passes away, and Waverly Funeral Home handles his arrangement. Waverly has an agreement with neobituary.com to post the obits of all its decedents (obituees). Neobituary posts Mr. Bacon's tribute. When Dwight Eier reads Mr. Bacon's online obit, he sees an ad for a company that will send a frozen lasagne to Mrs. Bacon—a little comfort food for the grieving family. When Mr. Eier clicks through and makes the purchase, Frank's Lasagne makes a sale, Mrs. Bacon gets a lasagne, and Neobituary and Waverly each receive a percentage of that sale.

Again, there's nothing dodgy about this arrangement. Ads on memorial sites save visitors the hassle of going elsewhere to buy or give. If it weren't for ads conveniently placed near obituaries and virtual memorials, many charitable gifts wouldn't be made at all (and perhaps fewer families would enjoy the gift of pasta).

It's hard to find fault with ads like this. But too many ads, or the wrong kind of ads, can be obnoxious. Some fly-by-night sites even urge families to establish funeral gift registries.

Virtual candles and flowers are often similar to Like buttons—you click the white lily, for example, to show you're thinking about the departed. That's cool. But other sites charge a steep fee for the privilege. Look, I'm all for capitalism. But paying to light a virtual candle or leave a virtual rose is the digital equivalent of buying a pet rock: Buyers receive little or nothing of real value in exchange for their money.

If you have cash to burn, by all means—light a candle for the low, low price of ten bucks a month. If you decide to keep it, you'll pay not $100…not $80…not even $59.99. If you light a perpetual candle today, you'll pay just $50! Hurry, offer ends soon. (Terms and conditions apply. See your webmaster and payday lender for details.)

Costs

Watch your pocketbook—or PayPal account, as the case may be—when you choose a memorial site. Memorial platforms profit from your content in several different ways. That's no sin—the death industry is a business, not a public service. But be aware of the possible costs before you choose a platform.

Reactivation Fees

Your loved one's free online obit won't remain publicly accessible forever. Eventually it's archived—that is, it's still indexed by search engines and will turn up in search results, but most of the text is placed behind a paywall and no longer freely accessible to readers. To see the obit behind the wall, you'll have to "sponsor" its reactivation.

Depending on the site, reactivation can cost $20 to $30 per year, or you can permanently sponsor an obit for about $80 (2017 prices). On some sites you can restore content temporarily by purchasing a 1-day access pass. The fee to remove the paywall is usually steepest in the first year after the obituary is archived, when grief is fresh and the family is more likely to unlock the content. A lower "maintenance" fee may be offered to incentivize subsequent renewals.

Some newspapers place the obits behind a soft paywall in their online editions—that is, readers have to pay after reading a certain number of obituaries. Techdirt suggests gatecrashing by turning off javascript, using different browsers (Chrome and Firefox, say) or dumping your cookies.[15]

Access to Premium Features

Most new offerings in the crowded digital memorial space give users free access to basic features, but require a fee for premiums like extra space and fancy presentation tools. For example, your free plan may allow you to post as few as three photos with the obituary. To upload more images or post video or audio files, you'll have to ante up some legal tender.

Some platforms charge a flat fee. Others require a recurring subscription that renews automatically unless you cancel. One-time-fee sites won't suck you dry year by year, but they cost more up front. You also risk committing to a site that flatlines in three months. (We'll talk more about permanence later in this chapter.) Always store your files in multiple locations.

Upgrades

In addition to paying hosting fees for server space, you may be nickeled-and-dimed with surcharges for incidentals: plug-ins, apps, swank templates, and so on. Check with the Better Business Bureau to be certain you know about all possible *Gotcha!* fees before you commit to a platform.

As recently as 2014, Americans were spending more than $420 million per year on obits.[16] Newspapers collected 75% of that windfall. Even with upcharges and unexpected fees, online memorials are a bargain compared with their newspaper counterparts. A typical print obit costs $250 to $900. Imagine how many memorial candles you could light with that kind of dough.

Privacy Issues and Control of Content

When you register to create a digital memorial, you must agree to the terms of use. Most of us skip the fine print and check the box without a second thought. But in doing so, you've probably just given the developers (the owners of the memorial site or app) complete control over your content and permission to access or "share" (sell) your personal details and contact information. In many cases, the terms also give the developer permission to police and censor your content.

Read the fine print. Watch for checkboxes that automatically sign you up for newsletters or secure your agreement to share information with the app's partners, which means anyone they decide to sell your information to.

Here's an example of the blanket agreement often found in the Terms of Use section. It gives the developer license to use any or all of your content and media in any way they wish:

> You grant Acme Memorials and its affiliates a royalty-free, perpetual, irrevocable, nonexclusive, transferrable right and license to use, copy, modify, display, archive, store, publish, transmit, perform, distribute, reproduce, and create derivative works from all material you provide in any form, media, software or technology of any kind now existing or developed in the future.

Criminee! Technically, you still own your material. But you've granted the developer such generous borrowing privileges that you might as well have given it away. If this is a deal breaker for you, buy a URL and build your own memorial.

Visibility

"The Internet is replacing the library, the newspaper, and the photo album," says Geoffrey Fowler, a personal technology blogger for the Wall Street Journal, "so what does it mean if Google doesn't know you were here—and that you're now gone?"[17] The visibility of a memorial page, whether it's for yourself or a loved one, depends on search engine optimization (SEO).

To rank well in a Google search—that is, to be optimized—the content of your memorial page must be indexed, so that a search engine can find it. When someone keys in, say, "obituary" and "Janis Joplin," the search engine's giant brain flips through its massive Rolodex of keywords and finds not only the 1970 obit for the rock 'n' roll icon, but also a mention of her in the obit for a man who died suddenly on his birthday:

> Those of you [who were] in attendance are asked to contact the Pope if you have a photo of the soiree that captures the image of St. Peter, St. Patrick, or Janis Joplin in the background, as it is not certain when our dear James "left" the gathering. *–James Felton Dunn (1929–2016)*

Finally, the better known the site, the more visits you'll get from those browsing other obits and memorials—what the Pew Research Center calls "incidental readership."[18] A DIY site is at a disadvantage because it's not part of a larger platform that will attract visitors. If you don't mind keeping a low profile, or if you feel confident you can build your own traffic on social media, don't be dissuaded by the light volume of accidental visitors.

Permanence

Will the content we post on the web really stay there forever? Jonathan Margolis, technology editor at the London-based *Financial Times,* is optimistic. "Digital archivism got off to a shaky start in the 1970s with changing software formats and hardware standards," he says. "But most of what we generate now should stick around."[19]

Looking at the stack of inaccessible 3.5-inch disks in my office closet, though, I have my doubts about the permanence of my digital footprint. We don't think of electronic information as being vulnerable to degradation or corruption, but digital archivists—librarians whose job it is to preserve content—say all those bits and bytes are fragile.

In addition to physical deterioration, information can be wiped out when a site goes belly up. Researcher Molly Kalan, in an interview on Peter Billingham's superb podcast *Death Goes Digital,* points out that sites like Facebook "don't have to keep those profiles up…there's' a false understanding that these things will be around for forever."[20] Using a memorial site "require[s] a leap of faith that the provider will continue to get new paying customers to keep the servers running."

Your content can be mothballed without warning. That's exactly what happened to customers of the photo storage app Picturelife. When the app went dark, customers who had stored their photos on the Picturelife server lost everything they had posted there if they had no backup. One customer, in an interview on the podcast *Reply All* (also one of my favorites) said he'd lost 93,000 photos going back more than 20 years.[21] Ironically, the app's tagline had been "Never worry about losing your pictures again." (Listen to podcast episode #71 for the happy ending to this mess.)

The moral of the story is that bankruptcy is forever, but your "lifetime" subscription may not be. You can't rely on any single app or website—memorial or otherwise—to house your content. Back it up to your hard drive, store it in the cloud, or both. See Chapter 9 for details on backing up and storing your media and other content.

Social Media Integration

Pews may be empty these days, but Twitter feeds and Facebook pages are well attended. Once you've created a digital memorial, share it on social media, such as Twitter, Reddit, Tumblr, Pinterest, or Instagram.

Some apps are designed to piggyback onto others. To integrate your site with Facebook, follow the instructions at developers.facebook.com. You can set up a Facebook login for your memorial, integrate Facebook comments, and more. You don't need to be a developer, and you don't have to have an app. Just copy and paste a few snippets of code. Facebook integration (as used, for example, by Infinibond) makes it easy for most people to access your site but skews your audience toward a younger group. Those who still read obits in the newspaper will be left out.

Design

The stuffy memorial templates currently on offer showcase the best design trends of 1997. They take their inspiration from mass cards and funeral programs. The site backgrounds are either anemic or shadowy, the preselected images clichéd and sappy, the music cheesy and glum, and the fonts, graphics, and layouts incredibly stale. And what's with that dreadful shade of greenish-yellow? *Ugh*.

An outmoded mindset about death and dying still prevails among memorial sites. People who create online obits want to celebrate a loved one's life, yet only a few memorial templates are clean and contemporary, much less cheerful and uplifting. Offering standout design seems like an easy way to edge out competitors, but the funeral industry—even the portion of it that's gone digital—is still giving us harps and angels.

Chapter 9

NEAR-TECH EXPERIENCE
Adding Images, Video, Audio, & Music

"People take more and more photos, but paradoxically, they become more and more disconnected from them," says computer scientist Kevin Quennesson.[1] Between the fish lips and food pics, it would be easy to draw that conclusion. But this chronicle of the
commonplace can probe our character in ways that were impossible before. "Facebook, Twitter and Instagram are increasingly where we go to process our inner thoughts and feelings about pretty much everything," says Katy Waldman, a tech writer for *Slate*.[2]

Regardless of its relative merits, digital media is here to stay. If you're reading this book, I'm betting you've embraced it. The key here is "digital": Before you can build your memorial, you'll need to collect, select, inventory, digitize, label, and edit your media assets—that is, your photos, videos, audio, and music. You might even want to create some new assets, such as voiceover narration or videotaped interviews. The complexity of this process depends on how much of your own media you have to sift through, how much you need to source from elsewhere, how much time you have to devote to the project, and how well organized and patient you are.

COLLECTING AND CHOOSING YOUR MEDIA

Sources of Images

Shoebox Photos

The scrapbooks my grandmother put together 70 years ago—my mother's baby book and my grandmother's own wedding album—are fragile now, their edges crumbling. As each year passes, that black-and-white world seems more remote and unreal—but also more magical. Most of us have photos like these—if not in albums, then in shoeboxes or (God help you) banker's boxes.

Cardboard or not, these boxes are treasure chests. Plunder them for photos to illustrate your obituee at every stage of his or her life. Look for shots of your obituee with various people and in various contexts. If you remove the photos from an album, use Post-Its or take careful notes so you can put the pics back in the same place after you've digitized them.

Social Media Postings

The best and most accessible source of photos and video of the obituee might be his or her own social media accounts. If you think your grandmother didn't use social media, you might be mistaken. Most of today's 75-year-olds were in the workforce 15 years ago. Your obituee could have used a computer for 10 years before heading to Boca del Vista. She might have whiled away many an hour poolside on Facebook.

You can also scour Google Images for photos. Use quotation marks around the obituee's name. Searching "James Kellogg" will find pages containing only that exact name.

Without the quotation marks, the search engine will pull every instance of "James" and every instance of "Kellogg." Search using several variations of the name, such as "James B. Kellogg" and "Jim Kellogg."

If you find an image you want to use, you can usually right-click it and save it as a picture (a JPG or PNG file). Alternatively, take a screenshot of the image and save that as a picture.

Pre-Planned Memorial Photos

Autobituarists are among the control freaks responsible for the popularity of "pre-planned memorial photography"—portraits made in anticipation of death. We anal-retentive types don't want to risk having a bad hair day for all eternity. When the time comes, a memorial photo is displayed on the casket or next to the urn containing the obituee's cremains. The image can also be baked into a ceramic cabochon attached to a headstone.

A memorial photograph is a modern take on the *memento mori*—the medieval Christian custom of making a death mask, keeping a lock of hair, or creating some other symbolic reminder that life is fleeting. The difference is that today's reminder is not an item representing a departed loved one, but an item representing ourselves. Somehow, a self-portrait seems a fitting symbol of death in this brave new iWorld of ours.

Postmortem Photos

Postmortem memento photography, also called "remembrance photography," is becoming widely used and available. Now I Lay Me Down to Sleep (NILMDTS) is a nonprofit organization that provides "the gift of professional portraiture" to parents of stillborn or at-risk infants. Most parents who have lost a child urge healthcare professionals to encourage memento photography even if parents are reluctant.[3]

Here are some other ideas for illustrating a child's obituary. They can be used alone or combined into a collage, gallery, or slideshow:

- Sonogram
- Inked footprints

- Pregnancy photos
- A favorite storybook or toy
- The child's baby quilt or blanket
- The child's name on the wall of his or her nursery

Stock Media

Stock photo agencies such as iStock, Dreamstime, Shutterstock, and Graphic Leftovers offer image collections, illustrations, video footage, and audio clips you can license for use on your memorial. Licensing an image is like buying it except that you lack exclusive rights—that is, others can purchase and use the same image.

The cost of licensing stock media depends on several variables, such as where you buy it and how you plan to use it. For example, you'd pay ten or fifteen bucks to license a still photo for use on a digital memorial. The price to reproduce that same image on a t-shirt or other item for resale, however, shoots north of $150.

Some agencies charge a premium for higher resolution (clarity). Many agencies group their best or most popular images into premium collections that cost more than standard stock. They may also use demand pricing—the more popular the image, the higher the price, just like an airline ticket. If you need to license several items, you can save by purchasing a subscription package or image bundle.

When you search for stock photos, use the wisdom of the crowd to your advantage: Search by "most popular" or "best selling." The most popular images are always the best in terms of quality and composition. If you search by the default option—"newest" or "most relevant"—you'll find yourself weeding through a thicket of corny, poor-quality shots. Later in this chapter, we'll discuss sources of public domain (free) images.

Sources of Documents, Art, and Mementos

In addition to photos of your obituee, you can enhance your memorial and preserve family history by including mementos.

Paper mementos, such as diplomas and passports, can be scanned. A three-dimensional object, such as a barbecue grill, can be photographed. The only requirement for subject matter is that the memento be meaningfully connected to your obituee:

- Maps
- Memes
- Artwork
- Invitations
- Sheet music
- Screenshots
- Telegrams or faxes
- Remembrance tattoos
- Greeting cards or letters
- Coins, stamps, or paper money
- Work uniform, badge, or union card
- Boy Scout or Girl Scout badges or pins
- A favorite anything: chair, socks, pen, dog
- Remembrance jewelry or a loved one wearing it
- The obituee's name on a memorial brick or bench
- A wedding ring, class ring, or other engraved jewelry
- Quotations (see, for example, Pamela Wante's Pinterest board "Remembering My Father")
- Pilot's wings, stethoscope, or some other tool of the obituee's trade
- The obituee's gravestone or a loved one placing flowers, a flag, or other items at the graveside
- The obituee's birth certificate, draft card, driver's license, or—better yet—a stamped passport
- His or her name spelled out in rose petals or river rocks, or etched in sand on a beach and photographed from above (search online for these services)
- Receipts for special items (for instance, I have a 1938 receipt for a bouquet my grandfather bought for my grandmother on their first anniversary)

- Pressed flowers (I have a flower from that bouquet!)
- Report cards, baby clothes, or books
- A letterman's sweater, pom-pons, athletic memorabilia, or pageant trophies
- A favorite recipe, especially one handwritten on a recipe card by the obituee
- Tickets of any kind (such as an airline boarding pass, Broadway theater ticket, Powerball card, or St. Louis Blues season pass)
- Oddball items (I have, for instance, a 75-year-old candle and decorative frosting, now crumbling, from my mom's first birthday cake! My husband says it's creepy.)

If you do include any item bearing personal information, be sure to obscure the social security number and other identifiers digitally or with masking tape or a Sharpie. Identity thieves are not above preying on dead people.

Sources of Video

On January 18, 2006, the New York Times published its first multimedia obituary.[4] This tribute, for humorist Art Buchwald, was produced before Buchwald's death, with his enthusiastic cooperation. The video opens with a quaint, vaguely defensive explanation of the new format by a *Times* spokesman. Then Buchwald appears on screen, looking ill yet unable to contain his glee at being in on this final joke: "Hi—I'm Art Buchwald," he exclaims, "And I just died!"

Comparing this lively video memorial with Buchwald's print obit, the winner was clear: the obituary as we knew it had jumped the shark. Since then, video has become an integral part of most virtual memorials. Let's look at some sources of memorial video.

Family Video

If you're lucky, you have plenty of footage of your loved one. If you're like me, on the other hand, you walked around for years with a video camera in your hand/purse/pocket and didn't think to record a single video of your obituee.

If you're building your own end-of-life memorial or preparing a digital memorial for a terminally ill or elderly loved one, it's not too late. Watch some video obituaries on YouTube to get some ideas. Then record some family videos for your site.

Video Tributes

Whether or not the obituee has died, video tributes from friends and family are a great addition to a memorial site. As you collect information for the text portion of your memorial, talk to people who know or knew your obituee. With their permission, record your interviews and post snippets of them on your memorial site, or integrate them into a video with other media.

Funeral Video

A funeral or memorial service can be livestreamed to those who can't attend in person. Then the recording can become part of the obituee's memorial page. You might think it unseemly to record a funeral on video, but such a recording becomes a priceless memento.

To record the service, you can use a smartphone or hire a professional videographer. Ask your mortuary director to help you arrange it. If you can't find a funeral videographer in your area, a local wedding videographer will be happy to do the job.

Drone Footage

When Jason "Grunt" Branch, of Sanford, Florida, died in October 2015, his buddies at the Leathernecks biker club formed a sort of chrome cortège snaking toward the cemetery. The procession was captured on film by a drone. This footage was combined with acoustic guitar music, images of Branch with friends and family—even an introductory voiceover passage by Ronald Reagan.

The mood of the finished YouTube video is understandably heavy, since Branch died at age 35 (in a motorcycle accident, according to news reports and social media posts). A video like this can stand alone as a videobituary or, as part of a digital memorial, it could be combined with warm words and bright music to celebrate Branch's life. "I've had a good time living," says Nick Nolte, "so I'm going to have a good time dying." I suspect a guy like Jason Branch would second that emotion.

Other Sources of Video

Look for caches of videotape (VHS, beta, and reel to reel) on shelves, in closets, and in attics and basements (with permission of the homeowner[s], of course). Check the obituee's social media posts for videos. Later in this chapter, we'll discuss sources of public domain (free) video.

If you're preparing your own memorial, consider recording video messages for your loved ones. Some apps, such as Safe Beyond, If I Die, and Dead Social, store video messages to be released either when you die or at some specified time thereafter (see Chapter 10 for details). You could record a message, for instance, to be released when or if your child becomes a parent.

Select Your Visual Media

Chances are, narrowing down your choices will be the real challenge in media selection, especially when it comes to photos. A good strategy is to choose the shots that best illustrate your obituary text.

Even if you plan an obit in which the media, rather than the text, is the star, write your obit or narration first and then choose media to illustrate it. That's how documentary producers work, and it makes for a more cohesive presentation.

Either way, look for photos that represent the obituee throughout her lifespan. Try to capture her in a variety of roles—high school athlete, daughter, entrepreneur, and so on. Fill in any gaps with public domain media, stock images, or the obituee's own mementos. For example, if you have no photos of your father in uniform, photograph the uniform itself if you still have it. Or illustrate his military service with a medal, flag, helmet, or relevant document, such as a military ID, draft notice, or personal correspondence.

Sources of Audio

So often we think tenderly about a departed loved one's voice. An audio recording of it can stand alone as a link on your memorial site, or you can incorporate the audio into a memorial video. Using the Ken Burns effect, explained in Chapter 10, you can add movement to a series of photos and layer in your audio as the voiceover.

You can also use sound effects ranging from the drip of a leaky faucet to the rattle of a jackhammer. In a later section, we'll outline public domain (free) sources of audio. Now let's talk about a few other sources.

Voice Mail Messages

That last voice mail might seem too precious to share with the world. But if you think no one else would be interested in listening to such a mundane message, you're mistaken. It's hard to think of a more poignant sound clip to include in a memorial, no matter how banal the content. Post it on your memorial as a standalone link, or—better yet—use the voicemail as the narration for photos of you and the obituee together.

Cassette Tapes

Today's pilot, sailor, soldier, or marine on deployment picks up a cell phone or logs on to Skype or Facetime to check in with his or her family. The best my folks could do when my dad went to Vietnam was to mail cassette recordings back and forth. Geez, Louise—what a hassle. But what a treasure to have tapes like that for your memorial.

Recorded Messages from Mourners

Some digital memorials enable mourners to record audio messages. This is a nifty way for friends and acquaintances to share memories of the obituee and offer the family their sympathy.

Select Your Audio Files

Once you've collected a mess of audiotapes and audio files, it's time to organize and label them. Listening to hours of audiotape is mind numbing. If you can recruit a family member or friend to help, your powers of persuasion are astounding. Quit your day job and start selling timeshares post haste.

Chances are, though, you'll have to rely on an app, rather than a humanoid, to transcribe your recordings. The results won't be terribly accurate, but you'll at least be able to review topics and conversations quickly in order to pinpoint those of interest for your memorial.

Sources of Music

Musical artists usually earn royalties on the music they compose or perform (there are exceptions, such as music created with public funds). Any music you don't own must be licensed from the copyright owner before you post it on your memorial site. Rights for music that's not in the public domain are categorized as either royalty free or commercial.

Royalty Free

Royalty-free works are music tracks you can license for use on a website or app, such as YouTube. You'll pay a one-time licensing fee to the copyright holder, rather than shelling out royalties every time the song is played. Alternatively, you can choose among the royalty-free tracks YouTube provides. To find them, upload a video to your channel first, and then click the musical note icon.

Likewise, video editing apps usually offer packs of permissions-cleared tracks. Some video editing apps, such as Splice, will even sync the music to your video automatically.

Most memorial platforms, too, supply a small selection of royalty-free music for your use. The memorial app or site developer licenses these tracks on its customers' behalf. But cue the violins—most of this dreck is like extra-depressing elevator music. If you weren't already sad, you will be after listening to it.

Commercial

It's pricey and often difficult for an individual to license a pop song—even (or especially) an old song, such as Louis Armstrong's "What a Wonderful World." Normally, a swanky rights agency represents the copyright holder—in this case, the copyright is probably owned by Louis Armstrong's estate, although his heirs might have sold the rights to a third party.

The agency then negotiates a deal with the licensee. Licensing fees are steep. In 2017 the minimum annual fee to license a song from BMI for use on a website was $358.[5] Since such robust fees are out of most individuals' reach, licensees are usually not people but entities, such as advertisers.

If you're determined to license a certain pop song, find the copyright holder's name in iTunes or on a recently published physical recording of the track. Then search online for the copyright holder's agent and email your request.

Sources of Public Domain Media

Hundreds of thousands of photos, art, documents, video, audio recordings, and music are in the public domain—in other words, they belong to the public. Using public domain media is a great way to anchor your memorial within the obituee's generational and cultural context. Let's say you have a photo of your obituee at bat in his Louisville Cardinals baseball uniform. To accompany this snapshot, you could use a clip of Jack Buck's infamous 1985 World Series play-by-play: "Go crazy, folks! Go crazy!" It's available at the Internet Archive (archive.org).

If you dig deep enough, you can find anything you need in the public domain. The possibilities are limited only by your imagination and your search terms. Double-check the copyright notice for each item before you post it.

Works enter the public domain in several ways:

1. **Works with an elapsed copyright.** The period of copyright protection on most works ends 50 years after the author or artist dies. At that point, the work enters the public domain—that is, it becomes public property. Audio recordings are an exception— check each work individually to determine whether it's in the public domain.

2. **Works funded by taxpayers.** Any work funded even in part by a public grant or created by public servants during the course of their duties belongs in the public domain from the beginning—your tax dollars at work. For example, NASA's recording of

Buzz Aldrin's moon landing can't be copyrighted and is available for download on NASA's website.

3. **Works shared by copyright holders.** "The web is a sharing extravaganza of people trusting each other with who they are," says Brewster Kahle, founder of the Internet Archive.[6] Many copyright holders agree to let others use their creative output for free. Such works are distributed under a Creative Commons (CC) license. A public domain license is the most permissive kind of CC license available.

Visual Media in the Public Domain

The New York Public Library has one of the largest collections of public domain media in the world. More than 700,000 digitized items, including photos, letters, illustrations, maps, videos, newspaper clippings, book covers, postcards, fashion plates, and diaries, are available at digitalcollections.nypl.org.[7]

At Wikimedia Commons, browse 40,000 public domain maps, artworks, photos, and videos.[8] Search "Featured images," "Quality images," or "Valued images" to find the best pics.

The Internet Archive has been around for 20 years, and it's evolved far beyond its original scope. In this hoard are more treasures than trash. The site, archive.org, now houses millions of free books, documents, films, news and other television broadcasts, old-time radio broadcasts, audio and video recordings, software, advertisements, and other curios.

For more public domain options, such as the 200,000 items in the Florida Memory Project, check Wikipedia under "Public domain image resources." Some of the sites listed offer remarkably high quality images—lifeofpix.com is a case in point.

Audio Clips and Music in the Public Domain

Thousands of public domain audio recordings and music files can be found online if you poke around a bit. Be sure to include "public domain" (in quotation marks) in your search query. The Library of Congress, for example, has an extensive collection of audio recordings and music. In fact, it offers 53 versions of "Amazing Grace"—including a rendition by The Man in Black

(Johnny Cash) and one by The King himself (Elvis), both supplied courtesy of Sony BMG Music Entertainment.

Visit the website of any military branch or government agency to find audio recordings. At marineband.marines.mil, for instance, you can download a wide range of instrumental music performed by the U.S. Marine [Corps] Band. Available recordings include "Taps" and "The Star-Spangled Banner."

Other Copyright Considerations

Most creative output—writing, art, and even things like architectural blueprints and software code—is considered to be intellectual property. It therefore enjoys copyright protection from the moment it comes into being. This protection remains in force for the life of the author or artist and for 50 years after his or her death. Audio recordings are an exception—they're subject to more stringent copyright protection.

Fair Use

The "fair use" principle allows you to reproduce, broadcast, play, or otherwise use small portions of a work without violating copyright. My use of obituary excerpts throughout this book is an example of fair use under the law. If I'd reproduced an entire obituary, I would have needed to request permission from the copyright holder (generally the author).

Credit Lines

If you do need to request permission, your licensing agreement may require you to credit the author using specific language, such as "Photo ©Janish Upadhyay." Even if you don't have to, it's courteous to acknowledge the source of any borrowed item. Here are a few sample credit lines:

(Photo courtesy of the New York Public Library.)

(Audio clip courtesy of the Library of Congress.)

(Video used with the kind permission of Barbara Rudolph, M.D.)

TAKING STOCK OF YOUR MEDIA

Now that you've pulled together a mash-up of shoebox photos, public domain resources, family videos, and other media, take a preliminary inventory to see which items are already in an electronic format and which need to be—and can be—digitized.

If you're short on time or not up for an admittedly tedious project, inventory and digitize only what you need now. Label everything, especially if someone else will be digitizing the media for you. Once everything has been converted, update your records, and label and date your electronic files. Return photos to their albums, birth certificates to file cabinets, and so on.

Inventory Your Visual Media

Count your photos and document their source, subject, format, condition, and retrieval location (such as a JPG filename or a physical storage area). Do the same for your videos. Note the length and recording speed of each video. Note the beginning and ending timecodes for the portions you intend to use (6:40:00, for instance, indicates that the clip begins 6 minutes and 40 seconds into the video).

Inventory Your Audio and Music Files

List the subject and source of each audio recording or music track, and note (or estimate) the date on which it was recorded. Total up the number of audio recordings you have and how many minutes of audio are on each tape. Document the recording speed, brand, and condition of each one. Cassette and reel-to-reel tapes are fragile and can degrade in extremes of any kind—heat, cold, humidity, or dryness. If you need expert help, search online for audio restoration services.

Add Metadata

"Metadata" sounds like a mathematical or philosophical term, prompting anyone with good sense to recoil. But it's not as intimidating as it sounds. *Meta–* is a Greek prefix meaning "behind." That's fitting, since metadata is info that hangs out behind the scenes, helping search engines and archivists retrieve relevant digital objects. Keywords, in fact, are a type of metadata.

There are two kinds of metadata: descriptive and technical. Descriptive metadata documents the content, author, and size of a digital object. If the object is an audio or video file, the metadata also tells you who's seen or heard on the tape, using first and last names as well as dates of birth and death, if known and applicable.

Technical metadata indicates when the object was created and last modified and which file format it's in. Our computers rely on metadata to identify and retrieve files. The info is either embedded within an image—using HTML tags, for instance—or documented in a separate file.

Track your metadata in a spreadsheet or table. "Recording metadata is an upfront investment of time," says audio preservation specialist Krista White.[9] But it's worth it, she says, "to help preserve these histories intact. It's going to make a big difference in 20 years, not to mention a hundred."

Alt Text and Tags

Search engine algorithms give preference to well-designed, easily indexed sites with sticky content—that is, content that keeps visitors engaged. If your page loads slowly and impatient visitors leave, the algorithm will note a high bounce rate. The bounce rate indicates the likelihood a visitor will vamoose after viewing only one page on your site.

Smart as they are, search engines such as Google, Bing, and Baidu can't yet reliably determine what's in a photo. The alt text and tags tell the search engine what it's seeing, so to speak. Alt text is a text-only alternative to an image—hence the name. You can see the alt text when you hover over the image. Tags are keywords that are associated with an image but don't necessarily describe it. They tend to be more conceptual. A photo of a World War II veteran might be labeled with tags such as "patriotism," "military," and "aging," for instance. Tags are invisible to site visitors.

It's a good idea to supply metadata for several reasons. First, alt text appears if an image won't load on the user's device. Second, some sitebuilders use the filename as the default title if alt text isn't supplied. Most important, metadata helps search engines find your site or page. Adding captions—another type of metadata—also bumps up your page ranking. Facebook says using captions extends video viewing time by 12% on average.[10]

Here's an example of a filename, alt text, tags, and a caption for the aforementioned WWII veteran's photo:

Filename: Rockaway H., Army portrait, 1942-06-02

Tags: aging, military, uniform, war, patriotism

Alt text: Official U.S. Army portrait of Pvt. Harold Rockaway (June 1942).

Caption (placed on screen beneath image): Near the beginning of World War II, when he was just 15 years old, Harry Rockaway lied about his age to enlist in the U.S. Army.

DIGITIZING OLDER MEDIA

Each type of analog medium requires a different digitization technique. Let's run through them.

Digitize Your Photos

File Formats and Resolution

"Resolution" simply means clarity. How crisp or fuzzy is the picture? You've probably tried to enlarge a photo and found that it turned into blurry grid—a low-resolution or pixelated image. A digital image is composed of tiny squares called *pixels*. On-screen display resolution is expressed in pixels per inch (ppi). To calculate ppi, divide the image size by the number of pixels. The more pixels you crowd into a given space, the higher the pixel density.

As pixel density increases, it becomes harder for the eye to discern individual pixels and easier for us to see fine details. In a quality image—one of at least 300 ppi—pixels are invisible. For a list of file formats, see HowtoWriteanOnlineObit.com.

On the other hand, images must be small enough to fit your page or template without slowing down its loading speed or exceeding any size limit imposed by your website or virtual memorial. Various factors affect image size. One is the number of colors in the image—not the number of colors you can see, but the number of colors supported by your file format. A GIF can handle only 256 colors, for instance, compared with the 16 million gradations supported by the JPG format. Bottom line:

- The smaller the image size, the lower the resolution (quality), but the faster it loads.
- The larger the image size, the sharper the resolution— but the longer it takes to load.

Scanning

A scanner is an input device that converts visual information into digital data. A flatbed scanner looks and works like a copy machine—in fact, most high-end copy machines have scanning capabilities. But the niftiest way to digitize your snapshots is with an app like PhotoScan, from Google Photos. Apps like these turn your phone into a scanner input device. The results are better than taking a picture of a picture, because the app automatically rotates the scanned image and corrects any glare. The app also scans faster than a flatbed.

Using a good flatbed will yield better-quality scans compared with using a scanner app, but it's hard to discern the difference on screen. If you're sending out your images to be digitized, spring for higher-resolution scans—for example, 600 ppi. If necessary, you can use web-builder tools or a separate app to compress a photo before you post it. But adding pixels to an image is like trying to replace thinning hair—it can be done, but the process is tedious and expensive.

If you don't own a scanner, check your local public library or ask around—you probably have a friend or relative who owns one you can use for a few hours. If you decide to buy a scanner, look for one with an output resolution of at least 300 ppi. At that optical density, you'll be able to admire every last one of your cousin Ari's hair plugs.

Review the specs carefully first to see if the scanner is compatible with your hardware (your laptop or desktop computer). Make sure you have on hand any cables, SD cards, or adapters you need to transfer images from the scanner to your computer. Buying a scanner with a document feeder is unnecessary, since photos must be placed individually on the scanner bed, but having a feeder may be useful for future projects.

A decent scanner will set you back $50-$100, depending mostly on the resolution. A unit that can scan film negatives and slides will cost a bit more, since negatives and slides must be scanned at very high resolution—2000 to 3000 ppi—in order to produce adequate on-screen clarity. That's because enlarging a negative or slide bumps up the size of the image area (height and width) without increasing the number of pixels that make up the image. With fewer pixels per square inch, image quality diminishes. Images must be scanned at very high resolution in order to compensate.

Digitization Services

To save yourself the hassle of all this, consider having your media professionally digitized. Businesses that specialize in photo or video scanning have sprung up recently. You can buy a package of, say, 250 scans for about what you'd pay for a flatbed. Here's how it works: You ship your photos to the scanning service in a trackable package. The service then scans your media and returns it along with digital files in your preferred format (such as archival DVD). You can then upload the image files to your memorial site, make prints, or use them however you like.

Copy stores will also scan your photos for a fee. It can be hefty—sometimes several bucks per scan—but the process is quick and painless. If the items are fragile, find a digital restoration specialist to repair or clean and restore them. A specialty service can recover audio and home movies from old technologies like VHS and beta for about $10 per tape.

If you want someone to take everything off your hands, full-service vendors like Everpresent will scan and organize your photos, audiotapes, and videos, put together a memorial video, and even write the obituary. Always check the Better Business Bureau's website before committing to a particular service.

Digitize Your Audio Files

Audio recordings may not survive long enough to be digitized. It's all too easy to record over or erase a tape. Unlabeled or mislabeled cassettes may be tossed in the garbage. The condition of the media may deteriorate. Cassette and reel-to-reel tapes, vinyl records, and wire recordings are subject to warping, mold and fungus, breakage, and shrinkage. The magnetic layer of sound information can peel away or flake off of its tape backing or stick to the player.[11]

In addition, incompatibilities with newer hardware may make it difficult to extract the sound information. Playback problems can also occur if a tape wasn't rewound properly.

If you need to digitize audio recordings that are in dubious condition, check the Audio Preservation and Restoration Directory offered by the Association for Recorded Sound Collections (ARSC). These experts can help you transfer, restore, or recover your files.

BACKING UP AND STORING

Back in the day, we were always just a keystroke away from disaster. An entire file could go *poof* with one false move. These days, once you have the right backup systems and settings in place—cloud storage, an external hard drive, and devices that sync to one another—you have to work at losing your files.

For any important file, follow the 3-2-1 rule:

> Keep three copies of the file on at least two different types of media (such as a USB stick, hard drive, and cloud storage), one of which is offsite (in the cloud or at another physical location).

Cloud storage is remote digital space on a network. Options include Apple iCloud, Microsoft OneDrive, Amazon Drive, Dropbox, Box, and Google Photo (which replaced Picasa). It's wise to opt for a paid plan, or the cloud server might automatically compress your files, degrading their quality.

Local storage is digital storage on the hard drive of your laptop or desktop computer or on a physical device that attaches directly to your computer, such as a USB stick or a DVD.

Many cloud storage apps sync locally. That means your media is saved simultaneously to the cloud and to the local storage device(s) you designate.

If you have hundreds or thousands of digitized photos, organize them with a photo manager. You'll be able to find what you need easily instead of interrupting yourself repeatedly to search for a particular image.

If you use a Mac or an iPhone (or both), try the iOS Photos app, which replaced iPhoto and Aperture. Microsoft dumped its lackluster Picture Manager app with the release of Office 2013 and no longer incorporates image editing software. However, many good alternatives, such as Adobe Lightroom, are available. Amazon Prime members receive unlimited photo storage on Amazon Drive (this storage isn't really free, since it requires a Prime subscription). You can access the images stored on Drive through the Amazon Prime Photos app.

Look for these features in a media manager:

- Offers a suite of photo editing tools
- Cost is low (but not necessarily free, as explained above)
- Lets you easily import, export, share, and delete photos
- Syncs across all your devices (for example, a photo taken with or uploaded to an iPhone will sync to your iPad or iPad mini, iPod Touch, Mac, and Apple TV)
- Organizes your photos into albums automatically by date, place, person, or other criteria, such as season or holiday
- Includes a powerful search function (for example, a search for "hats" will automatically pull together every pic in which a person is wearing a hat)
- Allows you to caption, tag, and label photos with names, dates, and other information (if you have, say, a wedding photo taken in Lake George, New York, on the fifth of October, 1963, use Wolfram Alpha to add

the day of the week [Saturday] and weather info [the temp climbed 40 degrees that day, from 30 degrees that morning to 70 degrees by late afternoon])

Take these steps before you get started:

1. If you're using a virtual memorial site or app, check to see how many photos you're allowed to upload. Upgrade to a premium plan if necessary to accommodate the number of images you anticipate using.

2. Note the acceptable file formats and size limits. Convert or compress your media if necessary.

3. Install all updates to your operating system.

4. Check your cloud storage capacity. Image and video files are large, and your space will fill up quickly.

5. If your backup depends on syncing your devices, be sure to use the same sign-in (username and password) on all of them.

Chapter 10

STYLE POINTS
Applying Filters & Special Effects

Image editing is the Wild West of the internet. Settlers scramble to claim new territory. But this gold rush can't possibly support all the hopeful developers who come to try their luck. New photo and video editing apps ride into town and are gone by sundown.

Corrections and enhancements, such as blemish removal and color adjustments, are old hat. New(-ish) editing options have a lot more razzmatazz. As you'll see in the following pages, it would be easy to get sidetracked trying to jazz up your images and videos. If your schedule is tight, confine your changes to practical edits, such as cropping and red-eye removal, or skip process entirely and upload your digitized photos and video clips sans modification.

PHOTO EDITING
If you do have the time, experimenting with editing apps is a fun way to spiff up your digital memorial.

Augmented Reality

In virtual reality, the user immerses himself in a computer-generated environment. Augmented reality (AR) is the opposite: it's produced by superimposing digital imagery onto the real world, or onto some representation of it (such as a photograph).

Creative uses for the technology may be developed in the future. For now, though, AR is limited to slapping mosaic eye shadow, ice crowns, and other blingy crapola onto our photos. AR filters can turn a male into a female or vice versa, age or reverse age a person, distort facial features, and so on. Or try selfie lenses, 3D illusions, and masks like those available in Facebook Masquerade.

Look, most of us wouldn't want to see our 82-year-old nana puking a rainbow in her obituary portrait, like the kids do in their selfies. But many social media users are young or middle-age adults. Forty-one percent of 18- to 34-year-olds use Snapchat every day,[1] and 55% of 18- to 29-year-olds are daily users of Instagram.[2] If your obituee was one of them, a set of rabbit ears might be just what he or she would've wanted. "Instagram's spin on Snapchat's selfie masks is designed to make them simple and less wacky so they appeal to users beyond teens,"[3] says TechCrunch analyst Josh Constine.

If your obituee was a fan, bring on the special effects. Just how special some of them are is debatable, but there's no question they give the formality of the traditional obit a long-overdue smack right in the kisser.

Surreality

The linguists at Merriam-Webster Dictionary chose "surreal," meaning "marked by the intense irrational reality of a dream," as the word of the year for 2016. Interest in the word surged that year after a terrorist attack in Belgium, a massacre in France, a coup attempt in Turkey, and the election of Donald J. Trump as president of the United States. [4] (For real.)

In the tech world, surreality is a sophisticated type of AR. These systems have in common the ability to project computer-generated images onto objects in the physical world. For example, virtual pictures and info about the deceased could appear on or near a real grave or headstone.

Surreality will undoubtedly open new frontiers in virtual memorialization. We'll be watching these advances in future editions of this book. In the meantime, get updates at HowtoWriteanOnlineObit.com, and follow me on the social media links there.

Illustration Effects

AR illustration effects, some of which we've already mentioned, are mad-popular. You can create them by adding textures, ink, stickers, or doodles to your snapshots or by adding images to layered shapes. Artfully applied, these effects can help you create simple overlays or high-concept photomontages to share in Snapchat, Instagram, What'sApp, Kik, and similar messaging apps. These assets can be components of a virtual memorial.

You can even create a geofenced sticker customized for a funeral or memorial service. The sticker is made available on the app (such as Snapchat) in a limited geographic area for a certain period of time. Snap users, for example, would then take a selfie or other pic at the service and overlay the custom geofenced sticker, which is essentially a digital photo frame.

The predesigned templates in Snapchat's prom and love categories work well for memorial stickers, but explore others, such as the waves sticker in the Summer Vibes category and the flowers options in the Wedding category. The big downside here is the cost. I'd have to cough up around $75 to create one measly geofenced sticker available within my small neighborhood for 1 hour (see my samples on HowtoWriteanOnlineObituary.com). Still, it's a swell idea to create a custom sticker for a funeral. When the obituee's friends send you photos using the filter, you can save them and upload them to the obituee's memorial page.

Filters

Art Filters

Art filters convert images into digital works of art, sometimes in the style of a particular artist and painting, such as Van Gogh's

Starry Night. A fragmentation filter creates an artistic effect by breaking an image into cubes or giving it a stained-glass or mosaic effect—a nice touch in a virtual memorial.

These filters are more restrained than, say, warping a human face to resemble an electrical outlet. In fact, applying an art filter to a pic or two is an easy way to make your virtual memorial more modern and intriguing.

Style Filters

A style filter digitally alters an image to create certain effects, such as a washed-out vintage look or a grainy, gritty urban vibe. Some style filters produce nostalgic, Polaroid-like images that work especially well in digital memorials.

Combined Images

Cloning

Cloning tools let you reproduce an image of an object or person—not necessarily in an identical position or pose—several times in a single scene. For instance, photos of a kid making a snow angel in three different positions could be layered onto a single snowy background.

Composites

A composite image combines two or more photos into one. For example, you could replace your aunt's stringy brisket with a beautiful roasted duck on the holiday table. This effect works with video, too—you could, for example, show Uncle Vinnie with an angel on one shoulder and a devil on the other.

Collages and Mood Boards

A collage is a collection of photos arranged in a grid or mosaic. It's often combined with text, a patterned background, and other decorative elements, such as hearts and flowers. Some social media apps supply tools for creating photo collages—Instagram Layout is an example.

A moodboard is an extension of this concept. It's a freeform collage centered on an emotion, person, or theme. It may include music, photos, letters, poetry, and other mementos. A moodboard can be imported into a virtual memorial, posted on Facebook, or shared in almost any other social medial platform.

A person with cancer might create a moodboard centered on her chemotherapy, for example. If she's creating an end-of-life review, this moodboard could become part of it. Or her obituarist could import the moodboard into a virtual memorial prepared after her death. In a way, a digital memorial is itself a moodboard focused on an obituee and interlaced with broad themes of grief, memory, and celebration.

You can create a DIY collage with Photoshop or similar software. Be sure to use the dimensions specified for the platform on which you plan to post the finished collage—for example, an Instagram collage must be 1080 x 1080 pixels.

An easier solution is to use your picture manager to create a collage—Google Photos, for instance, has built-in collage tools—or download a collage editor like PicStitch, PicMonkey Collage, or BeFunky. Some apps will even arrange your images into shapes, such as globes, maps, jigsaw puzzles, or pyramids.

Looped Images

Instagram offers Boomerangs—short strings of images looped together to create a Vine–like GIF or meme. Snapchat now offers a similar feature as part of Stories. Many other apps and picture managers, including iCloud Photos, have looping animation tools. For example, I combined images from my folks' fiftieth wedding anniversary party to make it look as if they're feeding each other a bite of cake.

Predictive Technology

What if you could take a single 70-year-old snapshot of your grandmother's birthday party and turn it into a video in which she blows out the candles on her cake? Computer scientists have devised a predictive algorithm that can set a scene like this into motion.[5]

To develop the technology, experts in artificial intelligence (AI) and machine learning at MIT fed 2 million videos into a computer and asked it to analyze events, sequences, objects, and settings. This analysis produced a massive data set that taught the algorithm to project scenes into the future. The system learned, for example, that trees stand still, glass breaks, and birds fly. It also learned the speed and characteristic motion of things that move—tricycles, taxicabs, people on sidewalks and escalators, children playing hopscotch.

Predictive video technology is still in its infancy, generating videos less than 2 seconds long, but soon it'll be possible to animate your memorial with video clips of long-ago scenes.

VIDEO EDITING

Making a memorial video is more like producing a documentary than a narrative film. In the latter, the script is the touchstone. The actors are cast, and the story unfolds in a fluid way that lets the audience forget it's not real.

In a documentary, on the other hand, real-life footage is the starting point. There is no script. The filmmaker doesn't necessarily even know how the story will play out. This authentic footage is then combined with photos, letters, documents, historical film, and whatever other oddments can be patched together to form a cohesive narrative. The process is more piecemeal than narrative filmmaking, and the outcome more a rustic quilt than a smooth fabric—it holds together and might even be beautiful, but there are a lot of ragged seams showing.

You'll use this documentary approach to create your memorial video. As an alternative, instead of preparing a single video, you could upload individual video segments to various parts of your memorial site.

It's tricky either way if you have little or no actual video footage of the obituee. You'll have to pattern a narrative from photos, archival footage, mementos, and interviews with those who knew him or her.

Techniques

If you do have video clips to work with, apps such as iMovie, Splice, Filmora, Videoshop, and Cameo can help you trim, combine, and sync them. You can add filters similar to those available for photos, incorporate music and voiceover narration, create subtitles, and share the finished video on YouTube, Vimeo, Facebook, or other channels, as well as on your memorial. Let's consider some basic video editing techniques.

Ken Burns Effect

The Ken Burns effect is a deceptively simple trick that gives cinematic movement to still photos. Instead of presenting a series of static shots, the way a slide projector does, this technique achieves the illusion of movement by panning across or zooming in on each image. For example, you might open with a full-length portrait of your parents on their wedding day, slowly zooming in on their joined hands before dissolving to the next image. Or you could pan across a photo of your brother's hockey team, lingering a moment on his face when you reach his position in the lineup.

This technique has become so familiar and popular that it's now the default setting for video editing platforms such as iMovie. It's hard to recall how innovative this method was when Burns introduced it in his documentary series *The Civil War* (1990). The technique, says Burns, is his attempt to "will old photographs alive."[6]

"The Kid Stays in the Picture" Effect

Advanced users might want to try a variation on the Ken Burns technique that allows you not only to pan and scan, but also to make objects in the foreground pop out in 3D. This method, named for the documentary in which it was first used, is known awkwardly as the "The Kid Stays in the Picture" effect.

Green Screen Background

Green-screen photography merges two videos by clipping out the subject of one and placing it on the background of another to create a composite. This is how those clever Madison Avenue types make commercials in which a living person (such as Natalie Cole) sings a duet with a deceased person (Nat King Cole). Using this technique, also known as chroma key compositing or the blue-screen effect, you could make the subject of your footage stand on the pitcher's mound in Yankee Stadium. A blue background is used if the subject of the clip is wearing green clothing, and vice versa. Free blue- or green-screen stock footage is available from the Internet Archive.

Picture-in-Picture

A picture-in-picture effect is useful in narrating your video (or a portion of it), showing two views of a scene at the same time, or revealing someone's reaction to what he's seeing on screen.

Slow Motion and Time Lapse

Many apps let you adjust the playback speed to create slow-mo or fast-forward effects.

Special Effects

Want to show your brother's barbecue grill exploding or steam coming out of your dad's ears? A broad range of animated special effects like these can be added to your video. Just be sure they enhance the narrative—don't use a particular animation just because you think it's a bad-ass effect.

Transitions

A transition is simply the way in which the video moves from one screen or scene to the next. Transitions change the viewer's perspective and advance the story. When transitions are used well, we don't even notice them.

Transition options, such as dissolve, flash, slide right, barn doors, and page curl, are built into every video editing program. In most apps, you simply drag the selected transition into your video timeline. It's best to choose one transition as your go-to, changing it only when the content gives you a reason to do so.

Transitions are especially important in memorial videos, which splice together bits and bobs of media in order to represent the obituee at various ages and in many different contexts and roles. A simple memorial video might dissolve from one photo to the next as a generic music track plays. An advanced production might use light leaks, lens flares, or any of a dozen other common video transition techniques. Stock agencies such as Shutterstock offer thousands of variations you can license for use in your video.

Dissolves

A "dissolve" is a transition in which one image slowly becomes transparent and disappears as another image becomes visible beneath the first. According to Christopher Bowen, co-author of a popular film-editing textbook, slow dissolves deliberately call attention to themselves. [7]

This kind of transition is best used when the overlapping images are visually similar—for instance, you might fade from a recent portrait of your obituee into similar portrait of her as a young woman (the face in the two images should be about the same size and in roughly the same position). A dissolve can also suggest a significant change in time or place while maintaining the continuity of the emotional content.[8] That perhaps explains the over-reliance on dissolves in memorial videos.

Cross-Cuts

A cross-cut jumps back and forth between two scenes, such as the two ends of a phone conversation. To use this technique creatively, you might show the obituee's older self talking to his younger self. If you don't have video of the deceased, use photos augmented with comic book–style captions to represent each end of the "conversation."

Cutaways

A cutaway is a shot in which the camera moves abruptly to something else before returning to the previous scene. You might cut away to show a flashback, for example, or to show what someone sees out the window.

In a memorial video, cutaways often show context or location. For example, you might cut to a street sign or to the exterior of a home. To show a 1950s context, you could cut away to archival footage of a girl with a hula hoop. To advance the story, you could repeatedly cut to B-roll tape (file footage) of historic events, such as the moon landing or the fall of the Berlin

Wall (see Chapter 9 for sources of public domain [free] historical video).

To keep your memorial video cohesive, it helps to stick with a theme for your cutaways. Show cutaways to fashions of the '50, '60s, '70s, and so on, for example, or to a series of cars representing each era, for example. Your viewers will catch on quickly to this narrative device.

Other Transitions

Adding fancy transitions is time consuming and requires decent tech skills. If you're so inclined, have at it. Be creative—how might you personalize the transitions in your video to reflect your obituee's hobbies, interests, and life experiences? If he enjoyed photography, for example, how about using photo negatives to mark transitions? If he loved to travel, you could use postcards from the obituee's own collection to move the narrative along. Likewise, maps help viewers follow the geographical narrative of your obituee's life. You can even give a map the Ken Burns treatment, panning and scanning over it and zooming in on a particular region or city. Or if your obituee liked poetry, you could mark each main transition with a line of poetry, until at last you pan over the entire poem from top to bottom, using the Ken Burns effect.

Subtitles and Other Text Overlays

Adding subtitles to any video on your memorial site is important, since many users watch with the sound off. It's easy to add titles or speech bubbles to a video. The Clips app for iOS users automatically creates subtitles, which it calls "live titles." You'll probably have to correct some transcription errors, but the app gives you a head start in captioning. Similar apps are available for Android users.

Use only one or two point sizes in your subtitles, and be sure the type is legible on a small screen. Stick to a single text color or two, and use a consistent typeface. Place text in short blocks, rather than stringing it all the way across the screen. Make sure it appears on screen long enough for viewers to read it.

844444888888

88

Sound Editing

Skillful use of narration and sound effects in a memorial video can make it richer and more engaging, especially if there's no accompanying music.

Ken Burns (Again)

Ken Burns, whose pan-and-scan videography techniques were groundbreaking, was also an innovator in sound editing techniques. In a 1990 *Washington Post* review, George Will praised Burns's documentary *The Civil War*. "Burns's film of the battlefields today, and the old photographs, are 'framed' by ambient sounds—hoofbeats, cannon, musketry, steamboat whistles," says Will. "The birds you hear are the kind that called at the times and places of battles...And the pictures are exquisitely married to words...from the letters and diaries of soldiers and citizens."[9]

If you have email, letters, or other correspondence from your obituee, quote from it in your narration. A sound effect here and there in s memorial video—a creaking hinge, say, or the rustle of autumn leaves—can work well if you don't overdo it. Need some inspiration? Great excuse to watch a Ken Burns video or two.

Narration

Good narration ties together items that would otherwise seem visually fragmented—footage of your obituee, photos, mementos, maps, and so on. It creates the narrative thread that you'll follow throughout the video. Each digital object you add to your narration strengthens the story and places people, events, and even emotions in context. Begin with lousy narration, and you're likely to end up with a superficial, sentimental story. Here are some tips for writing good narration and incorporating it into a memorial video:

- **Format your script.** To create your script, you need a way to organize words, visual media, and sound. I suggest beginning with a multicolumn table on a horizontally oriented page. Number each row, and place the narration at left, a description of the visual media at right, and music/sound in the next column (leave the two media columns blank until you've filled in your narration). If you like, add a final column for comments such as "Need to track down" or "Mute sound in video."

An alternative is to use a brainstorming app, particularly if you invested in a good one while you were preparing to write your draft (see Chapter 5). These apps make it easy to shuffle media from one scene to another and to resequence the scenes themselves. This kind of script is more like a storyboard than a table.

- **Think about timing.** You can always trim a video or linger on an image, but you can't stretch a video. Time your media and voiceover to coincide in length. (If you like, use a separate column to indicate length.)

- **Read everything out loud.** Reading aloud is even more important in narration than in an online obit. You'll notice that your sentences sound stiff without contractions. You'll see that using a word like "individual" instead of "person" makes you sound like a police officer. And wordy phrases like "provided me with" (rather than "gave me") will be easier to spot.

- **Keep your audience in mind (see Chapter 2)**. Use language, humor, and cultural references your audience will understand and appreciate.

- **Use a consistent perspective.** See Chapter 3 for a description of first, second, and third person. Choose one voice and use it throughout your narration.

- **Be flexible.** Break up chunks of dialogue, move things around, and scrap anything that's not working.

- **Use layers to add depth.** Strategically stack music, narration, and the occasional sound effect, rather than alternating between or among them. If your video has sound, you can either use it or mute it and instead use some combination of music, sound effects, and narration. Use fewer layers if there's too much going on.

- **Tell a story.** Begin with the most exciting part of your story—that's your hook. Sandwich vivid details into the middle, and either leave us choked up with genuine emotion at the end or go out with a *Shazam!*—a bold quotation, maybe, or a hauntingly lovely image.

- **Create new digital assets to fill in the gaps.** If you've combed through your family videos, shoebox photos, and other media but can't find images to illustrate certain parts of your story, you'll have to hustle. Go out and interview the obituee's barber or manicurist on camera. Record some family stories. Search public domain sources of video and photos. Give the viewer a tour of the obituee's apartment or classroom or shoe repair shop.

- **Use best practices.** Don't try to depict the obituee's life from cradle to grave. Use specific language. Offer sensory details. Incorporate quotations. And by all means, make us laugh.

Posting Your Video

Uploading Video

Building your memorial on Facebook or a dedicated virtual memorial site simplifies video uploads for those who aren't familiar with the process. Just click the upload button, browse to locate the file you want to use, and click OK.

If you're not using a memorial template, you'll need to upload your video to a platform that can host and play it. such as YouTube or Vimeo. You can then embed it or link to it on your memorial. In other words, the video is housed elsewhere—on YouTube, for example—but played on your memorial site.

Before you can upload a video to YouTube, you'll be prompted to create a YouTube channel. A channel is simply a list of videos under your account name. The list can consist of a single video or hundreds of them. If you don't want anyone else to watch your channel, you can change the settings to make your content visible only to you and those you designate.

Using an Existing Video from Another Site

To use an existing video, such as archival film, download it and use a video editing app to trim and clip the portions you want to use, either as standalone video links or as part of your memorial video.

To link to an existing video, such as a funeral video on the mortuary's website, copy the embed code and paste it into your site. You can usually find the code by clicking the corner of the video or the Share link. Then paste the code into a video link or HTML text window on your memorial site. A widget will appear—it looks like a thumbnail image of your YouTube page—showing that your video is now embedded on your memorial site.

If necessary, resize the widget with your mouse. (Click, hold, and drag one of the handles along the edge.) If you like, move the widget to a different part of the screen. (Hover your mouse over the widget until you see a four-pointed arrow. Click, hold, and drag the widget to a new position.) Don't forget to save your changes!

Check the Support section of your player for other options, such as playing a video automatically or using a time stamp to start at a particular point in the video. If you have trouble, chances are that dozens of others have had it, too, and have posted the solution in a forum, blog, or article. Google the issue to find those discussions, or check the Help section of your platform.

MUSIC FOR YOUR MEMORIAL

Musical accompaniment for an obituary or memorial—or for any video posted on there—is optional. About 65% of obituarists choose to use music.[10] Facebook reports, however, that 80% of visitors are annoyed when music or other audio plays automatically.[11] We can't have the boss knowing we're not slogging through those TPS reports now, can we?

A better option is to notify visitors that a song is attached, and let them click to listen if they wish. See, for example, the 2016 memorial for 22-year-old Lisa Marie Andreana, which gives visitors the option of listening to a piano recording in which the performer is the obituee herself.

If you do opt to include music, use one of the generic tracks in your site's audio library, browse the royalty-free music on sites like Jamendo and IMA Tunes, or scout some public domain tracks, which offer a more original mix but aren't as easy to search or preview. Choose music consistent with your images. Keep in mind your overall site design and the obituee's age and personality, too. See Chapter 8 for more info on finding the right music for your memorial.

—

LAST RITES

What would your obituee have thought about the tribute you've prepared? Would she agree with your appraisal of her life? Would she be humbled that you've put so much thought into it? You might feel as if you haven't captured everything there is to say about your obituee (or yourself, if you're writing your own send-off). Remember, though, that even the most eloquent obit or media-rich memorial will fall short of human memory. On the screen, we can capture no more than a few pixels of the multifaceted person whose every word and gesture we knew. Why bother, then? We do it because there's something deeply satisfying about constructing a remembrance from the building materials of someone's life: stories, video clips, music, photos, and—if you're lucky—that last voice mail he left you.

What will people remember about you? We're still among the living. Every day is an opportunity to marvel at our good fortune, comfort the grieving, care for young and old, uplift those who need a hand, strengthen our relationships, make amends, pursue our dreams, and bring our respective life stories to some neat conclusion. History professor Jennifer Ratner-Rosenhagen sums things up nicely: "Neither we nor some almighty God are going to have the last word. It will be left to some schlubby mortals to make meaning of our mean lives."[12]

If this book was helpful to you, please consider reviewing it on Amazon, Goodreads, or elsewhere. Reviews help others find the book and help me improve it. To share your thoughts with me directly, please email melissa@HowtoWriteanOnlineObit.com. Thank you!

REFERENCES

CHAPTER 1

[1] Phillips J: The changing presentation of death in the obituary. *OMEGA* 55(4):325, 2007.

[2] Ghosh P: *Max Weber and the Protestant Ethic.* New York, 2014, Oxford University Press.

[3] Pew Religious Landscape Study: America's changing religious landscape: Christians decline sharply as share of population; unaffiliated and other faiths continue to grow. Pew Research Center for Religion and Public Life, Pew Charitable Trusts, 2014.

[4] Dawkins R: *A Devil's Chaplain: Reflections on Hope, Lies, Science, and Love.* New York, 2004, Marine Books.

[5] Staff writer [anonymous]: Greeting cards: The American way of death. *The Economist,* 29 June 2013.

6 Span P: Avoiding the call to hospice. *New York Times* New Old Age blog. 26 May 2009.

7 Staff writer: 2015 NFDA cremation and burial report, National Funeral Directors Association, 20 July 2015.

8 Hill A: Reality TV: *Audiences and Factual Television*. London, 2005, Routledge.

9 Zinsser W: *Writing About Your Life*. New York, 2004, Avalon.

10 Bennett L: The first-person industrial complex. Slate, September 1, 2015.

11 Google Trends: Oversharing. www.google.com/trends/explore#q=oversharing

12 Lock S: How to do it: Write an obituary for the BMJ. *BMJ* 311:680, 1995.

13 Katz J: Birth of a digital nation, *Wired*, 1 April 1997.

14 Anderson M, Perrin A: 13% of Americans don't use the internet. Who are they? Pew Research Center Factank, 7 September 2016.

15 Sweeney M: Newspapers face up to the ad crunch in print and digital. *The Guardian*, 18 October 2015.

16 Arntfield M: eMemoriam: Digital necrologies, virtual remembrance, and the question of permanence. In *Digital Death: Mortality and Beyond in the Online Age*. Santa Barbara, 2014, Praeger.

CHAPTER 2

1 Fowler B: Collective memory and forgetting: Components for a study of obituaries. *Theory, Culture & Society*. 22(6): 53, 2005.

[2] Haneman B: On the writing and reading of obituaries. *Medical Journal of Australia*, vol. 174, 1 January 2001.

[3] Keillor G: Onward and upward. GarrisonKeillor.com 17 February 2009.

[4] Zampaglione T, Bennett R: Electronically preserving obituaries. Public Libraries Online, 26 April 2013.

[5] O'Neill A: Funny obits bring new life to a dying art. CNN. In *CDI Funeral News*, 9 July 2013.

[6] See Zampaglione and Bennett, above.

[7] Mickey T, Warshaw B: Letters to the dead, Memory Motel podcast, 4 May 2016.

[8] McCollum H: The death of the free obit. *American Journalism Review*, April 1999.

[9] McElroy K: You must remember this: Obituaries and the civil rights movement. *Journal of Black Studies*, 3 April 2013.

[10] Johnson M: *Dead beat: Lost souls, lucky stiffs, and the perverse pleasures of obituaries.* New York, 2007, Harper Perennial.

[11] Kleinfield NR: The lonely death of George Bell. *New York Times*, 17 October 2015.

CHAPTER 3

[1] Talese G: Mr. Bad News: A profile of *New York Times* obituary writer Alden Whitman. *Esquire*, February 1966.

[2] Singer M: The death beat. *New Yorker*, 8 July 2002.

[3] Snicket L: *Horseradish: Bitter Truths You Can't Avoid.* New York, 2007, Harper Collins.

[4] Labella M: Columnist's obituary writing class draws national attention. *Washington Times,* 30 May 2016.

[5] Zinsser W: *Writing About Your Life.* New York, 2004, Avalon.

[6] Staley E: Messaging the dead: Social network sites and theologies of afterlife. In *Digital Death: Mortality and Beyond in the Online Age.* Santa Barbara, Calif., 2014, Praeger.

[7] Lam B: The inadvertent grief counselor. *The Atlantic,* 16 February 2016.

[8] Starck N: *Life After Death: The Art of the Obituary.* Melbourne, 2006, Melbourne University Publishing.

[9] See Talese, above.

[10] Lock S: How to do it: Write an obituary for the BMJ. *BMJ* 311:680, 1995.

[11] Hancocks S: View from the chair: Sadly missed. *British Dental Journal* 194(176), 2003.

[12] Braswell S: Are you ready to write your own obituary? *OZY,* 19 March 2016.

[13] LaBella M: Columnist's class on obituary writing draws national attention. *Eagle-Tribune,* 16 May 2016.

[14] See Braswell, above.

[15] See Labella, above.

[16] Welsh J: Guest editorial: What happens when a live wire hits the dead beat? Studs Terkel and the challenge of obituary writing. *Journal of Popular Culture*, 42(2): 215, 2009.

[17] Thomas RM and Calhoun C, editor: *52 McGs.: The Best Obituaries from Legendary New York Times Reporter Robert McG. Thomas*. New York, 2008, Scribner.

CHAPTER 4

[1] Gianotti G: What the study of voice recognition in normal subjects and brain-damaged patients tells us about models of familiar people recognition. *Neuropsychologia*. Epub 2011 May 4.

[2] Herz RS: The role of odor-evoked memory in psychological and physiological health. *Brain Sciences*, 19 July 2016.

[3] Zinsser W: *Writing About Your Life*. New York, 2004, Avalon.

CHAPTER 5

[1] Rosenthal R: Barf draft with an iPhone. HowSound podcast, 2 February 2015. **Note:** Producer Bradley Campbell credits the "barf draft" technique to reporter Rhitu Chatterjee.

[2] Samuelson A: *With Hemingway: A Year in Key West and Cuba*, New York, 1984, Random House.

[3] Zinsser W: *On Writing Well*. New York, 2001, HarperCollins.

[4] Alexa: Website traffic statistics for legacy.com, alexa.com/siteinfo/legacy.com.

[5] Nielsen J: How little do users read? Nielsen Norman Group, 6 May 2008.

6 Staff writer: Writing for the web. Usability.gov, U.S. Department of Health and Human Services, 15 June 2017.

7 Manuel T: The content corner: Will you read this entire post? Digital.gov, 11 April 2016.

8 Darlene Smith-Worthington, Sue Jefferson: *Technical Writing for Success*. Cengage Learning, 2011.

9 Mesbah HM: The impact of linear vs nonlinear listening to radio news on recall and comprehension, *J Radio Studies*, 10 June 2010.

10 Flaherty F: *The Elements of Story*. HarperCollins: New York, 2009.

11 Westbrook M: Take back the tributes: Getting rid of "in lieu of." *Magazine of the Society of American Florists (SAF)*, April 2015.

12 Staff writer: The wild bunch. *The Economist*, December 20, 2014.

13 Clark P: Forget flowers: A mortician breaks into sympathy food. *Bloomberg*, 9 August 2013.

14 U.S. Bureau of Labor Statistics: 2014 Consumer Expenditure Survey. Available at data.bls.gov.

15 Rahim Z: Here's how much people are expected to spend on Valentine's Day. *Fortune*, 7 February 2017.

16 Staff writer: BBC does not pay for flowers for staff funerals. *The Telegraph*, 17 August 2009.

17 Field B: In defense of flowers. *This Week at UCSD*, 14 Feb 2005.

CHAPTER 6

1 Braswell S: Are you ready to write your own obituary? OZY, 19 March 2016.

[2] Martin S: The top 10 obituary myths. *J-Source* (Canadian Journalism Project), 29 June 2016.

[3] McSherry M: Odes to lives. *Chicago Tribune*, 8 March 2008.

[4] Westbury C and others: Telling the world's least funny jokes: On the quantification of humor as entropy. *Journal of Memory and Language*, vol. 86, January 2016.

[5] Lewis D: Finally there's a scientific theory for why some words are funny. *Smithsonian*, 7 December 2015.

[6] Lock S: Write an obituary for the BMJ. *British Medical Journal*, 9 September 1995.

[7] King S: *On Writing: A Memoir of the Craft*. New York, 2000, Scribner.

[8] Rothman L: Why I am proudly, strongly, and happily in favor of adverbs. *The Atlantic*, 1 December 2011.

[9] Crum M: In defense of adverbs. Huffington Post, 6 May 2014.

[10] Flaherty F: *The Elements of Story*. New York, 2009, HarperCollins.

[11] See Flaherty, above.

CHAPTER 7

[1] Perelman School of Medicine at the University of Pennsylvania: Organ donation: 10 minutes. 22 people. 54 percent. *ScienceDaily*, 10 April 2017.

[2] Siminoff L and others: Consent to organ donation: a review. *Progress in Transplantation*, February 28, 2013.

[3] Staff Writer: Cremation favoured over burial by Britons, says poll. BBC, 18 April 2016.

[4] Cremation Society of Great Britain: www.srgw.info/CremSoc.

[5] Federa A: What writing obituaries taught them about life. PRI's *The World*. 31 December 2015.

[6] Sand E, Gordon KH, Bresin K: The impact of specifying suicide as the cause of death in an obituary. *Crisis* 34(1), January 2013.

[7] Weiss J and others: Stigma, self-blame, and satisfaction with care among patients with lung cancer. *J Psychosoc Oncol* 8:0 (ePub ahead of print), September 2016.

[8] Staff writer: "How would you like to handle the suicide in the memorial service or obituary?" Canadian Association for Suicide Prevention, www.suicideprevention.ca, 10 April 2015.

[9] Taylor B: The factor we can't forget when we discuss suicide prevention. The Mighty, 17 October 2016.

[10] Rudd RA and others: Increases in drug and opioid overdose deaths — United States, 2000–2014. *Morbidity and Mortality Weekly Report*, 64(50);1378-82, 1 January 2016.

[11] Rudd RA and others: Increases in drug and opioid-involved overdose deaths—United States, 2010–2015. Centers for Disease Control and Prevention: *MMWR*, 30 December 2016.

[12] NHTSA: Traffic fatalities up sharply in 2015. National Highway Traffic Safety Administration, 29 August 2016.

[13] Seelye KQ: Obituaries shed euphemisms to chronicle toll of heroin. *New York Times*, 11 July 2015.

[14] Kochanek KD and others: Deaths: Final data for 2014. *National Vital Statistics Reports*, 65(4), U.S. Centers for Disease Control and Prevention, 30 June 2016.

[15] Kersting A, Wagner B: Complicated grief after perinatal loss. *Dialogues Clin Neurosci*, 14(2): 187, June 2012.

[16] Gold KJ and others: Internet message boards for pregnancy loss: who's on-line and why? *Womens Health Issues*, 22(1): e67, January 2012.

[17] Phillips J: The changing presentation of death in the obituary. *OMEGA* 55(4):325, 2007.

[18] See Kochanek, above.

[19] See Kochanek, above.

[20] Flake L: Saying Goodbye to my mother: Peace after Alzheimer's disease. Loveofdixie.com, 3 August 2013.

[21] Ziants S: Saturday diary: I still can't write my mom's obit. *Pittsburgh Post-Gazette*, 2 January 2016.

[22] GLAAD: Accelerating Acceptance 2017: A Harris Poll survey of Americans' acceptance of LGBTQ people. November 2016.

[23] Brown A: 5 key findings about LGBT Americans. Pew Research Center Factank, 15 June 2017.

[24] See GLAAD, above.

[25] Meerwijk EL, Sevelius JM: Transgender population size in the United States: A meta-regression of population-based probability samples. *American Journal of Public Health*, February 2017.

[26] Kanamori Y and others: A comparison between self-identified evangelical Christians' and nonreligious persons' attitudes toward transgender persons. *Psychology of Sexual Orientation and Gender Diversity*, Vol 4(1), March 2017.

[27] My comparison of search terms "gender identity" and "sexual orientation" on Google Trends: Interest over time. 20 June 2017.

[28] James SE and other: The report of the 2015 U.S. transgender survey. Washington, D.C., 2016, National Center for Transgender Equality.

[29] Broom J: My husband's obituary: The life of Mark Robert Koepke. *Nuomo Huomo*. 19 March 2016.

[30] Pittelli R: When your abuser dies: Funerals, obituaries, and condolences. www.luke173ministries.org [undated entry].

[31] Grinberg E: Why angry obits go viral. CNN, 20 January 2016.

[32] Bullamore T: It's never been a better time to die: A look at the changing art of obituary writing. *British Medical Journal,* 26 July 2003.

[33] LeTrent S: Death of an unloved one. CNN, 24 September 2013.

[34] Oliphant M: *Marjoribanks: A Novel.* New York, 1867, Harper & Brothers.

[35] Obituaries from Coryell County, Texas. From an unknown newspaper published in Hamilton, Texas. November 1930.

[36] Johnson M: *Dead Beat: Lost Souls, Lucky Stiffs, and the Perverse Pleasures of Obituaries.* New York, 2007, Harper Perennial.

[37] Schmidt RH: *Sages, Seers, and Saints.* New York, 2015, Morehouse Publishing.

CHAPTER 8

[1] Honore C: *In Praise of Slowness: Challenging the Cult of Speed,* New York, HarperCollins, 2004.

[2] Raz NZ: Creating a "Memontage" for your digital legacy (interview). Death Goes Digital Podcast, Episode 17, 5 December 2016.

[3] Hill M: RipCemetery app wants to be the world's first virtual graveyard. Gizmodo, 10 February 2015.

[4] Jean PP, Woods VA: Estate planning for the digital afterlife. *New York Law Journal,* 10 November 2016.

[5] Moses L: 'We're looking for mistresses': How obit site Legacy combats trolling the deceased. Digiday, 18 January 2016.

[6] Alzheimer's Association Fiscal Year 2016 Annual Report. alz.org, June 2016.

[7] Staff writer: NFDA releases results of 2015 Member General Price List Survey, National Funeral Directors Association, 1 October 2015.

[8] Staff writer: Design for death architecture. Design Boom, 21 October 2013.

[9] Staff writer: What are mindclones? Lifenaut, 4 October 2013.

[10] Staff writer: U.S. newspaper affiliates [interactive map]. Legacy.com, 9 April 2017.

[11] Great Hill Partners: Press release: Great Hill Partners announces sale of Legacy.com to Pamplona Capital, 29 March 2017.

[12] Legacy.com: About us. www.legacy.com [undated].

[13] Staff writer: Online obituary business is booming. *Advertising Age,* 6 July 2016.

[14] Moses L: How Legacy.com is turning obits into business. Digiday, 4 September 2015.

[15] Masnick M: A paywall…for obituaries? TechDirt 14 July 2010.

[16] Marszalek D: Could newspapers be billion dollar biz for publishers? NetNewsCheck: The Business of Local Digital Media, 11 December 2014.

[17] Fowler GA: Online memorial services: after a death, celebrating a life online. *Wall Street Journal,* 28 January 2014.

[18] Barthel M: Newspapers: Fact sheet, Pew Research Center, 15 June 2016.

[19] Margolis J: Little sign of life stirring at virtual cemeteries: What will academics 1,500 years from now draw on as evidence of life in 2016? *Financial Times,* 28 February 2016.

[20] Kalan M: How is grief and bereavement expressed on Facebook? (interview.) Death Goes Digital Podcast, Episode 10, 20 June 2016.

[21] Reply All podcast, episode #71: The Picture Taker, 27 July 2016.

CHAPTER 9

[1] Newton C: Out of the picture: why the world's best photo startup is going out of business. The Verge, 5 November 2013.

[2] Waldman K: RT if you're :(about someone dying. Slate, 1 November 2013.

[3] Blood C, Cacciatore J: Best practice in bereavement photography after perinatal death. *BMC Psychology,* 23 June 2014.

[4] McDonald B and others, producers: Art Buchwald: The Last Word. *New York Times,* 18 January 2006.

[5] BMI: Digital licensing FAQ. BMI.com, 12 April 2017.

[6] Evangelista B: Internet Archive, repository of modern culture, turns 20. *San Francisco Chronicle,* 28 October 2016.

[7] New York Public Library Digital Collections: Public domain picks. digitalcollections.nypl..org

[8] Wikimedia Commons: commons.wikimedia.org/wiki/Main_Page

[9] White K: From cassette to cloud: Reformatting audiotape. YouTube webinar, 2 May 2016.

[10] Peterson T: Facebook will start automatically captioning video ads. *Advertising Age,* 10 February 2016.

[11] See White, above.

CHAPTER 10

[1] Read A: Why Snapchat Memories will be pivotal (and why marketers are so excited), Buffer Social, 27 July 2016.

[2] Duggan M: The demographics of social media users. Pew Research Center: Internet & Technology, 19 August 2015.

[3] Constine J: Instagram launches selfie filters, copying the last big Snapchat feature. TechCrunch, 16 May 2017.

[4] Young RD: 'Surreal' declared Merriam-Webster's 2016 word of the year, Reuters, Chicago, 22 December 2016.

[5] Furness D: MIT algorithm can predict the (immediate) future from still images, Digital Trends, November 28, 2016.

[6] Roston T: Ken Burns on "the Ken Burns effect" (and the 8 effects he actually uses), POV, 12 September 2014.

[7] Bowen C, Thompson R: *Grammar of the Shot*, third edition, New York, 2013, Taylor and Francis.

[8] See Bowen, above.

[9] Will G: A masterpiece on the Civil War, *Washington Post*, 20 September 1990.

[10] Fowler GA: Online memorial services: After a death, celebrating a life online, *Wall Street Journal*, 28 January 2014.

[11] Facebook Business: Capture attention with updated features for video ads. Facebook, 15 February 2017.

[12] Ratner-Rosenhagen J: Over our dead bodies, *Dissent*, Winter 2014.

44838894R00111

Made in the USA
Middletown, DE
10 May 2019